THE
NEEDLEPOINT
~ HOME ~
COLLECTION

THE NEEDLEPOINT HOME COLLECTION

with designs by

STELLA EDWARDS, KELLY FLETCHER

SANDRA HARDY, CHRISTINA MARSH

AND MARCIA PARKINSON

MEREHURST

NOTES
Some of the needlepoint designs in this book are very detailed and
due to space limitations, the charts may be shown on a
comparatively small scale; in such cases, readers may find it helpful
to have the particular chart with which they are currently working
enlarged on a photocopier.

First published in 1998 by Merehurst Limited
Ferry House, 51-57 Lacy Road, Putney, London SW15 1PR

Text on pages 16-23, 46-49, 82-87, 96-99 and 102-105 © Copyright 1998
Stella Edwards
Text on pages 38-45, 60-63, 66-69, 76-79 and 122-127 © Copyright 1998
Kelly Fletcher
All other text © Copyright 1998 Merehurst Limited
Photography and illustrations © Copyright 1998 Merehurst Limited

ISBN 1 85391 641 2

A catalogue record of this book is available from the British Library.

Designed by Mason Linklater
Edited by Diana Lodge
Photography by Michelle Garrett
Illustrations by King and King
Charts on pages 14, 52-53, 56-57, 75 and 121 by Clive Dorman and Co.
Colour separation by Bright Arts (HK) Limited
Printed in Singapore by C. S. Graphics

CONTENTS

INTRODUCTION

~

The art of needlepoint began to be popular about two hundred years

ago, when ladies embroidered designs copied from woven tapestries

onto canvas fabric. The origins of this type of embroidery may have

been imitative, but the resulting fabric turned out to be ideal for any

number of purposes in the home. As upholstered furniture became

popular, needlepoint proved to be immensely durable and hard-

wearing and was used for chairs, cushions, footstools, fire screens, pole

screens, tiebacks and trimmings. Available in a vast range extending

from the subtlest shades of green to bright reds and yellows, crewel and

tapestry wools offered an enticing and inspirational lure to designers.

The Needlepoint Home Collection

In recent years needlepoint has enjoyed a huge revival in popularity and there is a wide and ever-increasing range of designs and projects to make, including kits that come complete with pre-printed canvases and the necessary yarns, as well as plain canvases, in a variety of mesh sizes, on which you can work patterns and designs of your own choice. The selection of colours in tapestry and crewel wools and in stranded cottons increases all the time, and by mixing colours and textures you can create all manner of designs and patterns.

In this book you will find both large and small projects to make for the home, ranging from cushions, footstools and a bell pull, to smaller items such as a trinket box, a needlecase, or an inset for a small key cupboard. Many of the designs can be adapted into other things: a flower might be taken from the foxglove design and repeated lengthwise to make a bell pull; herbs could be taken from the herbal pillow for pin cushions or scented sachets, or the bluebell picture could be set into a box lid or a footstool.

Each design comes complete with a chart and a detailed list of all the yarns and other materials required. At the back of the book is a section for newcomers to needlepoint, detailing the basic skills and stitches. We hope that you enjoy re-creating a selection of the designs in these pages, and adding your own personal touch to each.

STELLA EDWARDS

Flowers are to be found everywhere – in gardens, window boxes, growing wild in the countryside, in bunches in shops, fresh or dried. They always bring cheer and happiness, and they provide me with one of the most pleasant forms of inspiration when I have to find new designs. There are so many different types of flower, and such a profusion of colours from which to choose, from the rich vibrant red of poppies to the deep purples and glorious yellows of irises, that it wasn't difficult to find subjects for six designs for this book.

I thought the most challenging aspect would be to select different projects, but this seemed to evolve naturally; for example, the morning glory is a climber, so its graceful twisting and climbing stems made it the obvious choice for a bell pull design.

Needlepoint is a most rewarding pastime, and there is so much that you can create. Not only is there the pleasure that comes from making something beautiful, but there is also the satisfaction of seeing the finished article and knowing that it will be admired for many years. As with gardening, you need patience, but when the plant grows and the flowers appear, whether in the garden or on canvas, you get an immense feeling of satisfaction.

KELLY FLETCHER

Having trained initially as a textile designer, I find myself naturally drawn to strong graphic imagery and repeat patterns. I enjoy creating designs that have a feeling of symmetry but which are never quite symmetrical. The smooth curves and jagged edges that are one of the features of tapestry are perfect for my colourful and highly patterned designs, and I like the way that even images that may look sophisticated on paper can suddenly appear to be almost naive when stitched.

My favourite subjects for designs are often traditional ones, such as animals and flowers, though I like to give them a more contemporary look by using patterned borders and backgrounds to add an extra dimension.

SANDRA HARDY

My particular style of needlepoint is not easily identifiable, as it seems to be a huge mixture of different styles, based on so many diverse influences and interests.

Teaching City & Guilds in soft furnishing and upholstery has no doubt contributed to my love of fabrics and stitched textiles, both old and new; while my design teaching concentrates on looking at patterns, shapes and colours and how they are interrelated. Many of my designs have a definite historical base, while others focus on present day images, but always with a striving to achieve something 'a little different'.

The creation of a design for a needlepoint project may start from a particular idea, but more often is sparked off by an everyday object, a visit to an exhibition or museum, or a picture in a magazine. It is always an exciting process deciding how to interpret a final drawing on the canvas, and which threads, colours and stitches to use. Backgrounds provide an additional design opportunity, so whenever possible subtle patterns or decorative stitches are worked.

When a design is completed, I am often surprised how different it is to the original drawings, but then remember all the 'trial and error', unpicking and experimenting that went on along the way!

CHRISTINA MARSH

I enjoy many forms of embroidery and it is always a pleasure to have an opportunity to design and stitch for canvaswork. As I am a keen artist and gardener it gave me great pleasure to design and stitch the iris book cover – and in my special book I shall keep planting details for my garden. I also find interior design very interesting and am always on the lookout for the latest trends; one current trend is the growing popularity of designs from the 1950s. The inspiration for my Summer Fruits tablemat and napkin ring came from this decade.

MARCIA PARKINSON

I use traditional designs as my starting point and develop my own versions while aiming to keep to the feel of the original. I begin a design by working out the pattern on graph paper so that the repeats and the scale suit the purpose of the finished piece of embroidery. At this stage, I am not concerned with colours – I just concentrate on getting the balance and complexity of the pattern right.

Once this is done, I start to build up the colours to get a rich composition that is true to the original inspiration, whether this is a rug, a religious artefact, an architectural detail, such as a painted panel, or even the general feel of a place.

Designing the projects for this book has allowed me to try out new ideas, such as the small box worked on plastic mesh and the cushion worked in rug wool on rug canvas. The designs I create for my company, Russell House Tapestries, always follow the theme of oriental rugs. For this book, I have widened the scope of my inspiration to encompass the textiles, architecture and environment of the middle east and north Africa.

ACCENTS FOR A PRETTY BEDROOM

The bedroom is a room in which you can indulge your individual style to the full. This charming collection – a trinket box, delicate picture frame, Victorian-style jewellery box, and a challenging picture for the skilled needlewoman – offers a chance to display your embroidery skills for your personal enjoyment.

TRINKET BOX

MARCIA PARKINSON

~

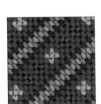

THE MOTIF ON THE TOP OF THIS BOX IS SIMILAR TO THE PATTERNS, LATER DEVELOPED INTO 'PAISLEY' DESIGNS, THAT ARE FOUND ON KASHMIRI SHAWLS FROM AROUND 1770-1800. IT IS THOUGHT THAT IN INDIAN DESIGNS THIS MOTIF ORIGINALLY REPRESENTED A FLOWER, BUT PERSIAN INFLUENCES AND WIDE-SPREAD USAGE CAUSED IT TO BECOME THOUGHT OF AS A CONE OR PINE. ALTHOUGH I HAVE NEVER BEEN FORTUNATE ENOUGH TO GO TO KASHMIR, I IMAGINE IT TO BE VERY VIBRANT AND RICH IN STRONG COLOURS, AND I HOPE I HAVE CAPTURED THIS VISION IN THE COLOURS USED FOR THIS BOX.

FINISHED SIZE

10 x 6.5 x 6.5 cm (4 x 2½ x 2½ in)

MATERIALS

35 x 27 cm (14 x 10½ in) of 10-gauge plastic canvas
No 22 tapestry needle
20 cm (8 in) strip of fine cotton lining fabric
A4 sheet of lightweight card
Tracing or greaseproof paper
PVA glue
Embroidery threads as given in the key

Opposite: the perfect container for pretty earrings or other little trinkets, this Indian-style box would make a lovely gift.

INSTRUCTIONS

1 Carefully count and cut the base and lid from plastic canvas, bearing in mind that each square on the graph represents a mesh intersection, not a hole. Trim stubs of plastic from the edges with small scissors.

2 Start to work the design from the middle, following the chart. Refer to the symbols on the chart and the key to find the correct wool colours. For soft cotton colours use half cross stitch; all other stitching is worked in cross stitch. Do not separate threads – use all strands together for full coverage (if you are using a thin metallic gold thread, you may require more than one thread in the needle to cover the canvas).

3 Using wine, oversew the edges together at corners to make the lid and base.

4 Make paper templates and cut base and lid sections from card and lining fabric. Use a blunt knife to score along the folds of the card base.

5 Lay the card base and lid sections on the wrong side of the appropriate fabric sections. Apply glue to the flaps, and bring them neatly over the card, mitring outer corners and cutting up to inner corners.

6 Carefully glue the fabric-covered linings into base and lid.

TRINKET BOX KEY

DMC embroidery threads

Perle cotton No 5

- ■   yellow 743 (1 skein)
- •   golden yellow 782 (1 skein)
- /   wine 814 (1 skein)

Metallic thread

- ↖   gold

Stranded cotton

- →   dark green 3051 (1 skein)
- ↑   light rose 223 (1 skein)

Soft cotton

- ☒   light green 3819 (1 skein)
- ❙❙   mustard 782 (1 skein)
- ▽   maroon 3685 (1 skein)
- S   dark rose 3803 (2 skeins)

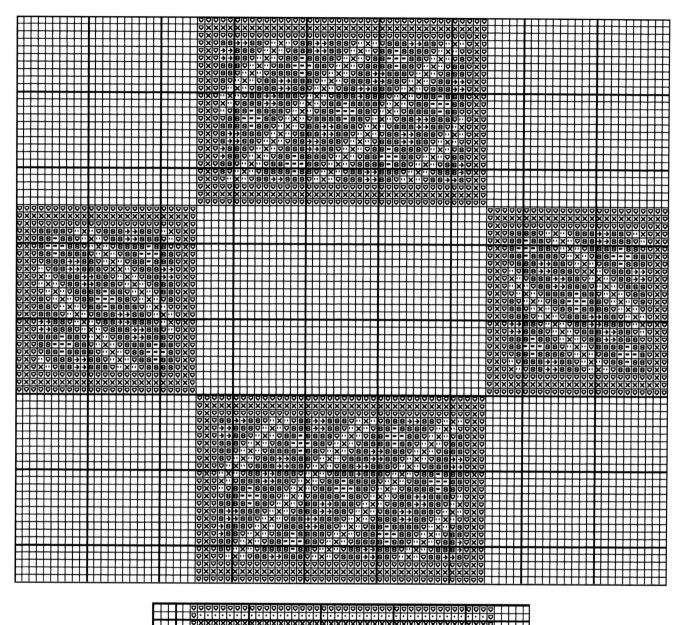

HERB PILLOW

STELLA EDWARDS

~

WITH A WEALTH OF HERBS AND SPICES FROM WHICH TO CHOOSE, I SELECTED A RANGE OF PINKS AND PURPLES, THEN ADDED A DASH OF YELLOW AT OPPOSITE CORNERS OF THIS PILLOW DESIGN. THE HERBS SHOWN ARE MARSH MALLOW, LAVENDER AND CHAMOMILE (ACROSS THE TOP), WITH BORAGE, CHIVES AND SAGE (ALONG THE BOTTOM). TO MAKE A SCENTED SACHET TO PUT INSIDE YOUR PILLOW, SIMPLY JOIN TWO SQUARES OF FINE COTTON AROUND THREE SIDES; TURN THE FABRIC RIGHT SIDE OUT; FILL WITH DRIED LAVENDER, AND THEN STITCH ACROSS THE GAP.

FINISHED SIZE

38 x 25 cm (15 x 10 in) approximately

MATERIALS

38 x 52 cm (15 x 21 in) of 10-gauge double-thread canvas

42.5 x 27.5cm (17 x 13 in) of backing fabric

40 x 25 cm (16 x 12 in) cushion pad

Dried lavender sachet

1.5 m (1¾ yds) of decorative cord

No 18 tapestry needle

Tapestry wool in the colours given in the key

Opposite: a collection of favourite garden herbs makes a delicate design for a bedroom; a sachet of dried lavender inside the pillow is a traditional recipe for a peaceful night's sleep.

INSTRUCTIONS

1 Embroider the design, using half cross stitch throughout. Start with the stem framework of the borders, then stitch from the centre of each motif. Finish with the cream background. Refer to the symbols on the chart and key to find the correct colours.

2 Press the embroidery on the back with a hot steam iron over a damp cloth and gently pull back into shape.

3 With right sides facing, sew the embroidery to the backing fabric, taking a 12 mm (½ in) seam allowance. Start about 12.5 cm (5 in) from one bottom corner and stitch to that corner, around the sides and top, and back to the bottom edge, leaving a gap of about 15 cm (6 in) at the bottom.

4 Trim back any excess canvas and fabric, cutting across corners at an angle to reduce bulk.

5 Turn the work right side out.

6 Fill the cover with the cushion pad, adding the lavender sachet, and stitch across the gap, leaving a small opening for the cord ends.

7 Stitch the decorative cord around the edges of the cushion, losing the ends in the opening.

HERB PILLOW KEY

Anchor Tapisserie wool

→   yellow 8016 (1 skein)

∕   pale pink 8392 (1 skein)

⌐   pink 8396 (1 skein*)

∖   bright pink 8452 (1 skein*)

✕   pinky purple 8488 (1 skein*)

−   pale purple 8526 (1 skein*)

∧   violet purple 8524 (1 skein*)

И   pale green 9094 (2 skeins)

V   sage green 9004 (2 skeins)

O   bottle green 8992 (1 skein)

S   dark green 9180 (1 skein)

I   red 8404 (1 skein*)

H   grass green 9006 (1 skein)

•   cream 8006 (10 skeins)

Note: you will only require short lengths of starred colours*.

LILY OF THE VALLEY FRAME

STELLA EDWARDS

THIS DELIGHTFUL FRAME IS SIMPLE TO EMBROIDER AND WOULD BE IDEAL FOR A SPECIAL PHOTOGRAPH OR PICTURE. THE BORDER OF SNOWDROPS AND PRETTY PINK AND BLUE RIBBONS LOOKS SOFT AGAINST THE CREAMY YELLOW BACKGROUND. THE SPACES IN THE LARGE WHITE DIAMONDS CAN BE FILLED WITH A NAME OR INITIALS, EITHER IN WOOL OR STITCHED OVER THE WOOL IN STRANDED COTTON. THE SMALLER DIAMOND AT THE BOTTOM HAS BEEN LEFT FOR A DATE TO RECORD THE OCCASION.

FINISHED SIZE

27.5 x 24 cm (11 x 9½ in) approximately, with an inset 16 x 11.5 cm (6½ x 4½ in)

Opposite: the delicate colours of this frame provide a charming surround to enhance a favourite picture.

MATERIALS

Note: the backing board should be sufficiently thick and firm to hold the fixings for hanging the picture; suitable fixings include screw eyes, threaded with picture hanging wire, or D-rings, which are attached to the back with small screws*.

38 x 33 cm (15 x 13 in) of 12-gauge interlock canvas

Mounting board, cut slightly smaller than the finished embroidery

Backing board, cut slightly smaller than the mount*

No 20 tapestry needle

Pretty lining fabric to back the frame

PVA glue

Strong thread and needle for lacing

Tapestry wool in the colours given in the key

INSTRUCTIONS

1 Follow the chart to work the design, starting in the middle of the top border and using half cross stitch throughout. Finish with the yellow background. Refer to the symbols on the chart and key to find the correct colours.

2 Press the embroidery on the back with a hot steam iron over a damp cloth and gently pull back into shape.

3 Take the slightly larger piece of mounting board and cut out the central aperture.

4 Cut diagonally from corner to corner both ways across the unworked canvas at the centre of the frame.

5 Spread the embroidery over the board and pin it to the edges of the board, pulling the canvas taut as you work.

6 Lace the canvas edges together at the back of the work, trimming away spare canvas if necessary.

7 Cut a piece of lining fabric to the size of the backing board, plus a 12 mm (½ in) allowance all around. Using PVA glue, cover one side of the board with the lining fabric, bringing the allowances to the back and gluing them in place.

8 Glue the board to the back of the frame along the sides and bottom edge (you can also neatly stitch these edges together, if preferred).

9 Slip your chosen picture into place through the gap at the top (if the picture is to be fixed permanently in the frame, you may find it simpler to glue it in place after step 6). Attach the fixings to the back of the board, and it is ready to be hung up.

LILY OF THE VALLEY FRAME KEY

Anchor Tapisserie wool

L	white 8000 (1 skein)
X	pale pink 8394 (2 skeins)
S	green 9018 (2 skeins)
•	yellow 8012 (3 skeins)
V	dark pink 8434 (1 skein*)
H	purple 8588 (1 skein*)
⌐	dark blue 8644 (1 skein*)
И	pale blue 8686 (1 skein*)

*Note: you will only require short lengths of starred colours**

BLUEBELL WOOD PICTURE

SANDRA HARDY

~

THIS PROJECT WAS INSPIRED BY MY LOCAL BLUEBELL WOODS, WHERE FOR A SHORT TIME EACH YEAR THE WOODS ARE TRANSFORMED INTO A GLORIOUS MASS OF COLOUR. THE FLOOR IS COVERED BY A CARPET OF PURPLE HUES, DAPPLED WITH SHAFTS OF SUNLIGHT, CONTRASTING SHARPLY WITH THE BRIGHT GREEN OF NEW BEECH LEAVES. THE FASCINATING DETAILS OF THE BLUEBELLS, WITH THEIR GRACEFULLY CURVING LINES AND DELIGHTFUL UPTURNED PETALS, HAVE BEEN PERFECTLY CAPTURED BY THE PETIT-POINT STITCHING ON THE DOUBLE CANVAS.

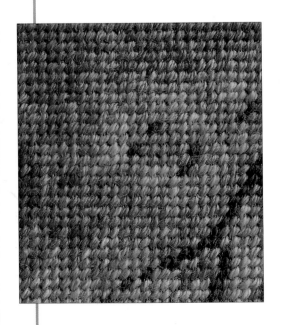

FINISHED SIZE

28.5 x 19.5 cm (11 x 7¾ in)

MATERIALS

40 x 30 cm (16 x 12 in) of white, 10-gauge double-
   thread canvas
Nos 20 and 24 tapestry needles
Tapestry wool in the colours given in the key
28.5 x 19.5 cm (11 x 7¾ in) of lightweight polyester
   wadding
Mount card and frame
Crochet cotton and large-eyed needle, for lacing

Opposite: the detailed petit point of the bluebell flower (charted separately on page 29) makes this picture an enjoyable challenge to stitch.

INSTRUCTIONS

1 Start by stitching the bluebell stalk, using one strand of wool and the size 24 needle and working half cross stitches over single canvas threads (petit point). The correct positioning of this stalk will make it relatively easy to place the bells.

2 Stitch all the petit point, including the filler stitches around the bell shapes, using the correct colours.

3 Stitch the background, working over double threads of canvas, using two strands of wool and the size 20 needle. Where two colours are named beside a symbol, use one strand of each. Stitch the beech leaves, then the bluebells in the foreground, and finally the remainder. Start at the top and work downwards to minimize the rubbing of existing stitches.

BLUEBELL WOOD KEY

Paterna Persian yarn

·I·	warm grey 256 (1 skein)
I	voilet 304 (1 skein)
●	grape 311 (1 skein)
♥	light grape 312 (1 skein)
S	plum 323 (1 skein)
~	very pale plum 326 (1 skein)
)	periwinkle 341 (1 skein)
◄►	fawn 404 (1 skein)
V	pale fawn 405 (1 skein)
◪	toast brown 472 (1 skein)
□	pale plum 321 (1 skein) and pale toast brown
X	pale toast brown 474 (1 skein)
◉	hunter green 611 (1 skein)
∩	pale hunter green 613 (1 skein)
▲	pale lavender and violet
★	strong khaki 642 (1 skein)
#	khaki 643 (1 skein)
Z	pale khaki 644 (1 skein)
J	very pale khaki 645 (1 skein)
∃	olive green 653 (1 skein)
△	lime green 673 (1 skein)
■	dark loden green 690 (1 skein)
+	loden green 693 (1 skein)
D	pale loden green 694 (1 skein)
-	very pale loden green 695 (1 skein)
ⅅ	butterscotch 704 (1 skein)
◇	old gold 755 (1 skein)
·	plum 327 (2 skeins)
◆	deep lavender 332 (2 skeins)
⊙	lavender 333 (2 skeins)
O	pale lavender 334 (2 skeins)

4 When completed, hold the canvas close up to a window so that any missed stitches can be easily seen.

5 Trim the canvas edges to 4 cm (1½ in) on all the sides, then press the back of the work with a hot steam iron over a damp cloth and gently pull back into shape.

6 Place the wrong side of the canvas over the polyester wadding, and then over the mount board or card.

7 Using the crochet cotton and large-eyed needle, lace the canvas over the card, making sure that the lines of stitching are parallel with the edges and mitring the corners to reduce excess bulk.

8 Either give the prepared embroidery to a professional picture framer, or cut an aperture of the correct size from coloured mounting board, using a craft knife, and insert the mount and embroidery into a purchased picture frame.

PETIT POINT KEY

I	voilet 304
●	grape 311
♥	light grape 312
~	very pale plum 326
◗	periwinkle 341
⋈	fawn 404
V	pale fawn 405
⊠	pale toast brown 474
★	strong khaki 642
Z	pale khaki 644
J	very pale khaki 645
+	loden green 693
−	very pale loden green 695
◁	butterscotch 704
·	plum 327
◆	deep lavender 332
⊙	lavender 333
O	pale lavender 334
·│·	warm grey 256
#	khaki 643
▱	pale loden green 694
◇	old gold 755

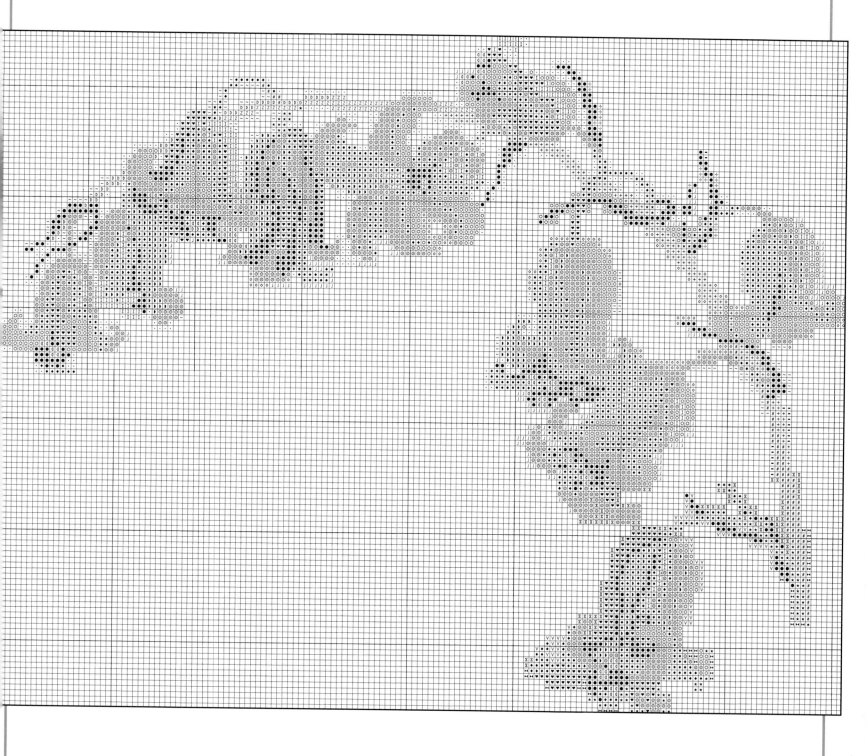

VICTORIAN JEWELLERY BOX

SANDRA HARDY

~

THE TRADITIONAL TECHNIQUE OF BEADING ON CANVAS WAS A FIRM FAVOURITE WITH VICTORIAN LADIES. HERE, THE SHINY, SPARKLY BEADS HAVE NOT ONLY HIGHLIGHTED SPECIFIC AREAS, BUT HAVE ALSO CREATED A UNIQUE TEXTURE TO THIS BRIGHT, FLORAL DESIGN, WHICH WAS INSPIRED BY SEVERAL LOVELY PIECES OF ITALIAN CERAMIC BROUGHT HOME FROM NAPLES.

FINISHED SIZE

31.5 x 41 cm (12½ x16 in)

MATERIALS

45 x 54 cm (17¾ x 21¼ in) of white, 13-gauge double-thread canvas
No 20 tapestry needle
Permanent marker pen
Tapestry wool in the colours given in the key
Seed beads as listed in the key
Beading needle
Polyester sewing thread, colour beige
31.5 x 41cm (12½ x 16 in) of lightweight polyester wadding
Staple gun and staples
37 x 20 cm (14½ x 11 in) cushion pad on a wooden box lid (for the suppliers of the box, see page 141)

Opposite: this large box, complete with interior compartments for earrings, bracelets, and necklaces, provides an ideal setting for a beaded canvaswork.

INSTRUCTIONS

1 Frame the canvas and and mark the positions of the three cream bands with a permanent (waterproof) pen. This will help you to locate the correct positions for the flowers and leaves.

2 Start stitching a bead panel, using double thread and the beading needle. Start with a knot a short distance away, and catch the thread around the canvas thread and through the knot for extra security, as shown.

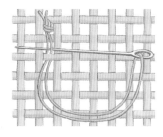

3 Using tent stitch, work complete rows of beading, not areas of colour as for needlepoint, starting at the top and working downwards, then stitch the other central panel.

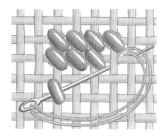

4 Stitch the stalks to the beads, using the tapestry wool and needle.

5 Complete the background of the beaded panels, alternating two stitches in one shade of blue with two in the other shade.

6 For the cream bands, stitch the inter-twining green lines first, and then fill in with the cream. Stitch all the leaves and flowers of the end panels, then the background.

7 Mark the centre sides of both the finished canvas and the lid. Place the canvas over the polyester wadding onto the calico pad, matching up the centre marks.

8 Staple these four points approximately 1cm away from the lid edges, pulling the canvas firmly, then staple from the centre towards each corner, placing staples approximately 2 cm (¾ in) apart.

9 At the corners, pull the canvas down in the centre and staple. Make two small pleats either side, and staple down, making the pleats as flat as possible. Trim away the excess canvas to within 1 cm (scant ½ in) of the staples, and attach the wooden lid by means of the screws provided.

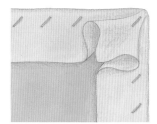

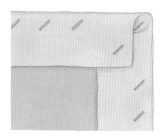

Anchor Tapisserie wool

·	white 8002 (1 skein)
S	old gold 8012 (1 skein)
E	autumn gold 8054 (1 skein)
∩	autumn tint 9534 (1 skein)
7	light spring green 9112 (1 skein)
Z	spring green 9114 (3 skeins)
⋈	laurel 9004 (3 skeins)
~	maize 8032 (5 skeins)
◆	light ancient blue 8734 (10 skeins)
▲	ancient blue 8736 (10 skeins)

Seed beads from Maple Textiles,
4.5gram (2mm diameter)

◺	yellow 050 (3 boxes)
J	iridescent yellow 053 (2 boxes)
∗	white 038 (2 boxes)
⊠	pale green 019 (2 boxes)
★	bright green 023 (2 boxes)
!	apricot 052 (1 box)
$	orange 054 (1 box)
♡	iridescent pink 039 (1 box)
■	dark green 020 (1 box)

Mill Hill seed beads

K	dark yellow 148T (1 box)

LIVING ROOM
COMFORTS

From its earliest beginnings, when embroiderers used tent stitch to

imitate the expensive tapestries that gave warmth and colour to the

walls of castles and country houses, needlepoint has been used to create

an ambience of luxurious comfort in the living room.

BIRDS IN A TREE

KELLY FLETCHER

 THERE'S AN AIR OF TRANQUILLITY ABOUT THIS DESIGN. THE SOFT COLOURS MAKE THE CURTAIN AND MATCHING TIEBACK IDEAL FOR A ROOM IN WHICH TO RELAX AND ENJOY SOME PEACE AND QUIET. THE CUSHION HAS NOT ONE BUT TWO BORDERS: AN INNER BORDER WITH A SUBTLE ZIGZAG DESIGN, AND AN OUTER FRAMEWORK OF LEAVES. THE CURTAIN TIEBACK IS DESIGNED TO COMPLEMENT RATHER THAN MATCH THE CUSHION, ELEMENTS FROM THE CUSHION BEING USED TO CREATE A MORE PATTERNED EFFECT.

FINISHED SIZE

Cushion 40 cm (16 in) square
Tieback 10.5 x 34 cm (4¼ x 13½ in)

MATERIALS (CUSHION)

60 cm (24 in) square of 10-gauge double-thread
 canvas
No 18 tapestry needle
50 cm (20 in) square of backing fabric to complement
 the needlepoint
45 cm (18 in) square cushion pad, for a well-filled
 effect
1.7 m (2 yd) of upholstery cord
Tapestry wool in the colours given in the key

Opposite: this restful design, with its gentle palette of soft colours has been used here for a tieback and a cushion cover, but the latter could equally well be set into a firescreen or footstool.

CUSHION KEY

Anchor Tapisserie wool

T	pale maize 8038	(1 skein)
▼	palest amber 8092	(4 skeins)
H	light amber 8094	(1 skein)
I	pale tangerine 8152	(1 skein)
•	palest terra cotta 8252	(8 skeins)
O	palest peaches and cream 8292	(1 skein)
3	old rose 8326	(1 skein)
Z	raspberry 8418	(1 skein)
Y	palest periwinkle 8602	(4 skeins)
←	cathedral blue 8786	(8 skeins)
K	jade 8966	(1 skein)
X	pale grey green 9064	(1 skein)
↖	palest apple green 9092	(2 skeins)
—	pale brown olive 9304	(1 skein)
⅃	palest granite 9772	(3 skeins)

If you are making the cushion and tieback, you will require the following quantities: 1 skein each of 8326, 8966, 9064 and 9304; 2 skeins each of 8038, 8094, 8152, 8292 and 8418; 3 skeins each of 9092 and 9772; 5 skeins each of 8092 and 8602; 8 skeins of 8252, and 9 skeins of 8786.

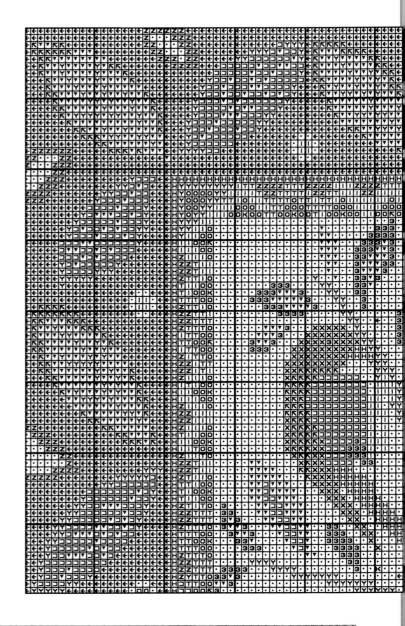

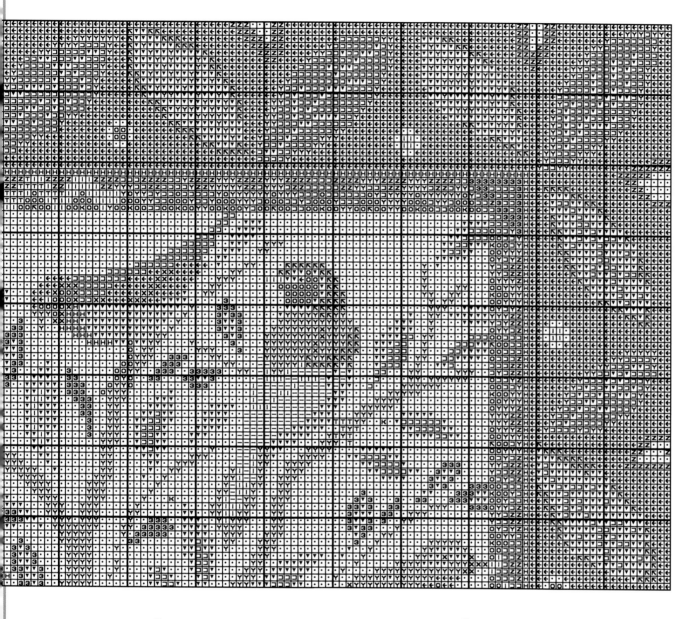

INSTRUCTIONS

1 Decide which part of the chart you would like to begin with. It's a good idea to start somewhere near the centre. Find the corresponding place on your blank canvas.

2 Thread your needle with wool no longer than 40cm (16 in). Each square on the chart represents one stitch over a double thread of the canvas. Following the chart, complete the design in half cross stitch.

3 When the design is completed, stretch the canvas if it has become distorted and allow it to dry before making it up.

4 To make a simple cushion cover, trim the unworked canvas to leave 2.5 cm (1 in) all around the edge of the stitched area. (For a zipped cushion cover, see page 59.)

5 With right sides facing, centre the canvas over the backing fabric, and pin and then baste three sides of the cushion to the backing fabric,

Cushion Key

T	pale maize 8038
▼	palest amber 8092
H	light amber 8094
I	pale tangerine 8152
•	palest terra cotta 8252
O	palest peaches and cream 8292
3	old rose 8326
Z	raspberry 8418
Y	palest periwinkle 8602
←	cathedral blue 8786
K	jade 8966
X	pale grey green 9064
⬉	palest apple green 9092
−	pale brown olive 9304
⅃	palest granite 9772

stitching as close to the needlepoint as possible. Turn the corners, but leave the bottom edge of the cushion unsewn.

6 Machine sew along the three basted edges; turn the canvas and fabric right sides out; insert the cushion pad, and hand stitch the fourth edge.

7 As a finishing touch, stitch upholstery cord around the edges of your cushion.

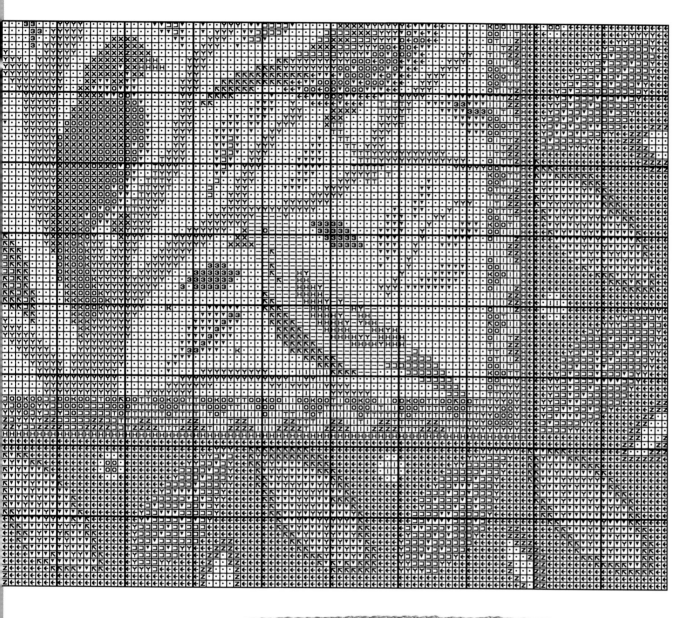

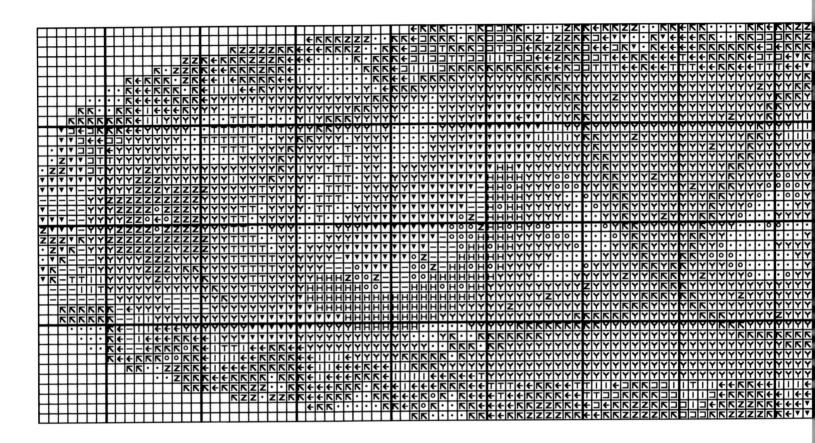

MATERIALS (TIEBACK)

20 x 46 cm (8 x 18 in) of 10-gauge double-thread canvas

No 18 tapestry needle

25 x 50 cm (10 x 20 in) of backing fabric to complement the
  needlepoint

1 m (1 yd) of upholstery cord

Tapestry wool in the colours given in the key

INSTRUCTIONS

1 Decide which part of the chart you would like to begin with. It's a good idea to start somewhere near the centre. Find the corresponding place on your blank canvas.

2 Thread your needle with wool no longer than 40 cm (16 in). Each square on the chart represents one stitch over a double-thread of the canvas. Following the chart, complete the design, using half cross stitch.

3 When the design is completed, stretch the canvas if it has become distorted and allow it to dry before making it up.

4 Trim the canvas edges to leave an allowance of 12 mm (½ in) around the stitching and cut the backing fabric to match.

5 With right sides together, stitch the embroidery to the backing fabric, leaving a gap at one end for turning. Turn the tieback right side out and stitch across the gap.

6 Stitch cord all around the edges of the tieback, forming a loop at each end.

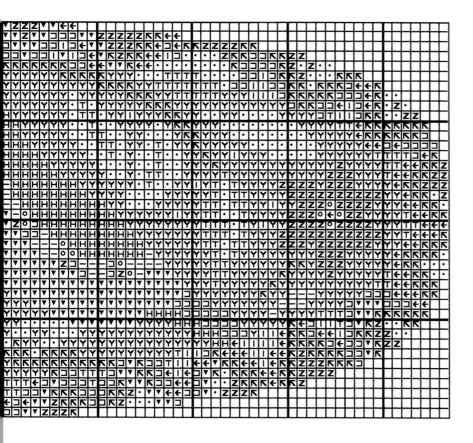

TIEBACK KEY

Anchor Tapisserie wool

T	pale maize 8038 (1 skein)
▼	palest amber 8092 (1 skein)
H	light amber 8094 (1 skein)
I	pale tangerine 8152 (1 skein)
•	palest terra cotta 8252 (1 skein)
O	palest peaches and cream 8292 (1 skein)
Z	raspberry 8418 (1 skein)
Y	palest periwinkle 8602 (2 skeins)
←	cathedral blue 8786 (1 skein)
⬈	palest apple green 9092 (1 skein)
—	pale brown olive 9304 (1 skein)
⅃	palest granite 9772 (1 skein)

MORNING GLORY BELL PULL

STELLA EDWARDS

~

BELL PULLS WERE VERY PRACTICAL IN THE LATE 19TH CENTURY, AS MOST HOUSEHOLDS EMPLOYED SERVANTS WHO WERE SUMMONED BY THE RINGING OF BELLS WHICH HUNG IN LONG ROWS IN THE SERVANTS' QUARTERS. FEW PEOPLE EMPLOY SERVANTS THESE DAYS, BUT BELL PULLS STILL LOOK MOST ATTRACTIVE IN 20TH-CENTURY ROOMS. THIS DESIGN IN PARTICULAR HAS A WONDERFULLY LUSH, TROPICAL FEEL TO IT. THE BEAUTIFUL BLUES OF THE MORNING GLORIES, WITH THEIR PINK DETAILS AND YELLOW CENTRES, LOOK STRIKING AGAINST THE GREENS OF THE LEAVES AND THE BLACK BACKGROUND.

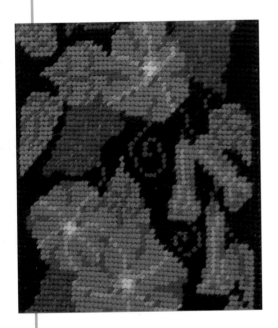

FINISHED SIZE

87 x 13.5 cm (35 x 5½ in) approximately

MATERIALS:

122.5 x 22.5 cm (49 x 9 in) of 10-gauge double-thread canvas

117.5 x 17.5 cm (47 x 7 in) of an appropriate backing fabric

No 20 tapestry needle

Tapestry wool in the colours given in the key

Bell pull fixings

Tassel

Opposite: black and other dark backgrounds were a great favourite with the Victorians, who appreciated the way in which they make colours glow.

INSTRUCTIONS:

1 Follow the chart to work the design. Instead of starting in the middle, it may be easier to start at the top left-hand corner of the design and work down. Use half cross stitch throughout. Stitch the design, then work two full repeats. Work a third repeat, leaving out the curved vine next to the blue flower at the bottom right-hand side. Add fifteen rows of black at the bottom of the design.

2 Press the embroidery on the back with a hot steam iron over a damp cloth and gently pull back into shape.

3 With right sides facing and stitching as close to the stitches as possible, sew the lining to the embroidery down the two long sides only.

4 Trim back any excess canvas and fabric along those edges, leaving 12 mm (½ in) allowances, and turn the work right side out.

5 Sew the bell pull fixings to the top and bottom of the bell pull.

6 Trim back any further excess canvas and lining; turn in the edges, and finish sewing across the two shorter edges of the bell pull.

7 Stitch a tassel to the bottom bell pull fixing.

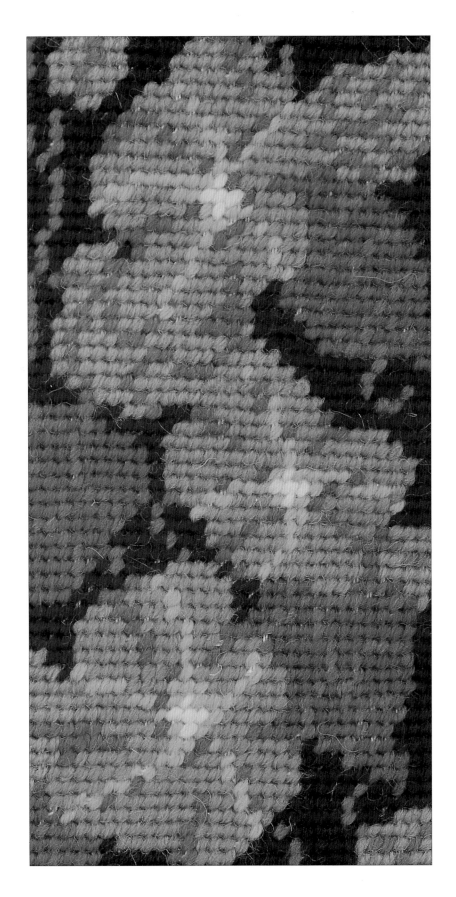

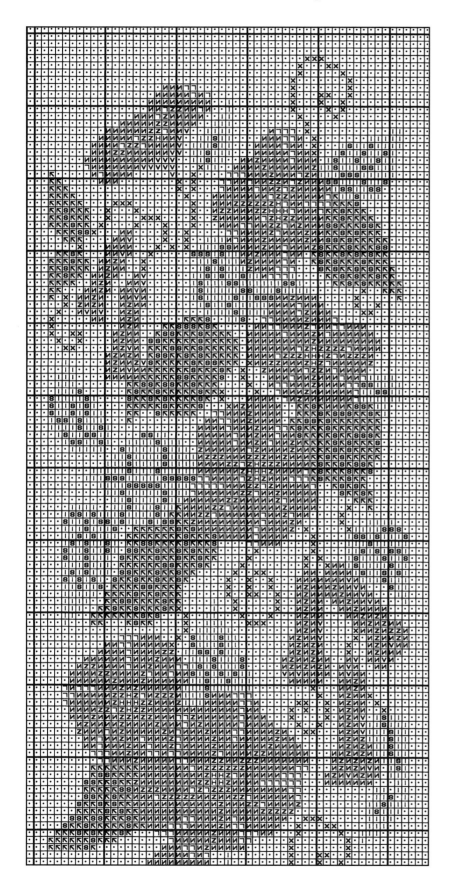

MORNING GLORY BELL PULL KEY

Anchor Tapisserie wool

И   china blue 8644 (4 skeins)

⌐   dark cornflower 8690 (1 skein)

H   pale yellow orange 8114 (1 skein)

Z   pale magenta 8486 (3 skeins)

V   dark magenta 8490 ((1 skein)

I   forest green 9018 (2 skeins)

S   laurel 9006 (2 skeins)

К   emerald 8990 (2 skeins)

X   moss green 9218 (1 skein)

•   black 9800 (10 skeins)

MARRAKECH BOX

MARCIA PARKINSON

~

THE PATTERN FOR THIS RICH NEEDLEPOINT IS BASED ON TRADITIONAL MOORISH TILES. THE DESIGN LOOKS COMPLICATED BUT IS VERY EASY TO FOLLOW IF YOU WORK ALL THE CHARCOAL STITCHES FIRST. THE REST IS THEN 'COLOURING IN'. THE PATTERN REPEAT CAN QUITE EASILY BE EXTENDED TO FIT ANY SIZE: MAKE A TEMPLATE OF THE REQUIRED SHAPE AND CENTRE THIS ON YOUR CANVAS, MAKING SURE THAT IT IS SQUARE TO THE WARP AND WEFT. DRAW AROUND IT, THEN STITCH OUT FROM THE CENTRE OF THE CANVAS, STARTING WITH THE CENTRE OF THE PATTERN MOTIF.

FINISHED SIZE:

30.5 cm x 21.5 cm (12 in x 8½ in)

MATERIALS:

40 x 30 cm (16 x 12 in) of 10-gauge mono cotton
   interlock canvas
No 22 tapestry needle
Tapestry wools in the colours given in the key
Box with upholstered lid (see page 141 for the
   address)
Staples and staplegun

Opposite: when stitching a repeat pattern, such as the box lid seen here, it is particularly helpful to start by drawing a pattern of grid lines on your canvas, using a waterproof marker.

INSTRUCTIONS

1 Every tenth line on the chart is heavier than the other lines on the grid (equivalent to every tenth line of holes of your canvas). If you are uncertain about working from the chart, you could mark every tenth line of holes of your canvas each way, using a waterproof (permanent) marker, so that the marks will not run and damage your finished embroidery.

2 Prepare and frame your canvas in the usual way, then start from a convenient central motif and stitch the design from the chart, using continental tent stitch. If you are using Paterna yarn you will need all three strands of wool in your needle.

3 When you have stitched the whole design, press the embroidery on the back with a hot steam iron over a damp cloth, then gently pull back into shape, stretching if necessary.

4 Neaten the canvas edges, leaving a generous allowance of unworked canvas around the embroidery, then either fit it to the prepared box lid, following steps 7–9 on page 32, or give it to a professional upholsterer to finish.

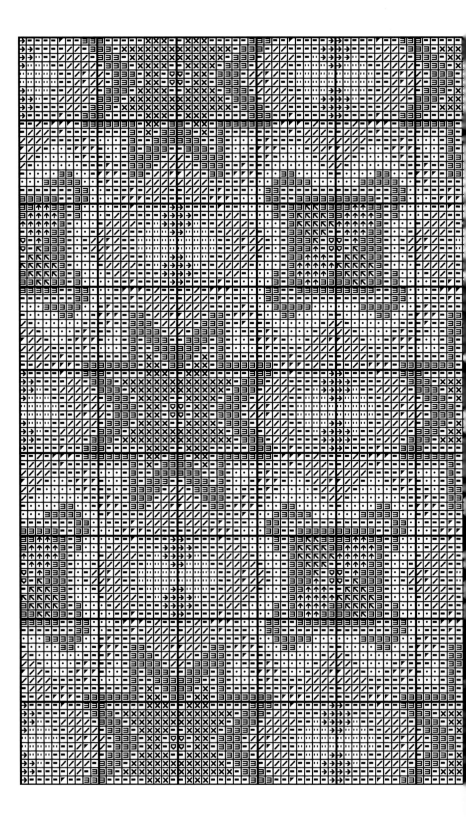

The Needlepoint Home Collection

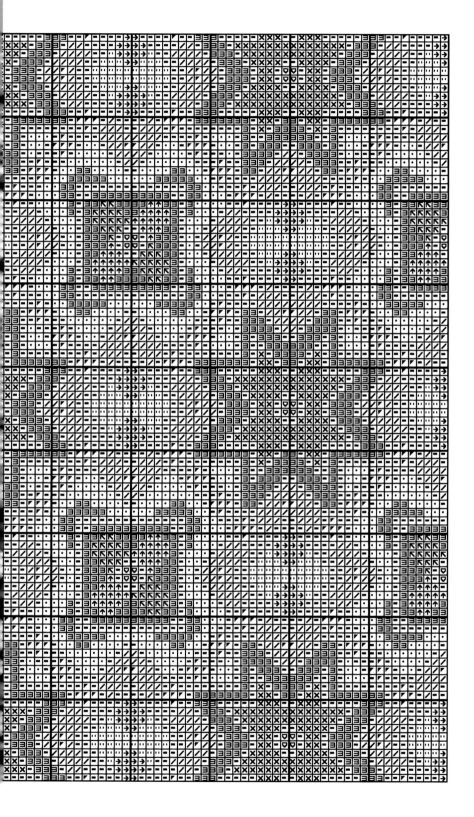

MARRAKECH BOX KEY

Paterna Persian yarn

- � black 220 (5 skeins)
- ⊡ dark gold 730 (2 skeins)
- ╱ dark blue 501 (3 skeins)
- ◰ dark sea blue 580 (1 skein)
- → dark green 660 (1 skein)
- ↑ wine 900 (1 skein)
- ✕ dark pink 910 (2 skeins)
- ⊟ purple 320 (1 skein)
- ▽ light gold 734 (1 skein)
- ⊒ bright green 661 (2 skeins)
- ◣ turquoise 663 (2 skeins)

KURD CUSHION

MARCIA PARKINSON

~

I HAVE CALLED THIS DESIGN 'KURD' THOUGH IT COULD WELL HAVE BEEN CALLED 'ARMENIAN' OR 'TURKISH' INSTEAD. USING TRADITIONAL COLOURS, I HAVE DEVELOPED THE PATTERN FROM THE TYPE OF CROSS-STAR MOTIFS THAT ARE OFTEN FOUND IN RUGS FROM THIS PART OF THE WORLD AND WHICH ARE USED IN BOTH CHRISTIAN AND ISLAMIC TEXTILES. THESE DESIGNS HAVE BEEN PRODUCED BY GENERATIONS OF NOMADIC WEAVERS WHO HAVE BEEN PUSHED AROUND THIS AREA BECAUSE OF POLITICAL UNREST AND UPHEAVAL.

FINISHED SIZE

Cover 42.5 cm (17 in) square, approximately; needlepoint 35.5 cm (14 in) square

MATERIALS:

50 cm (20 in) square of 13-gauge cotton interlock
   canvas
No 22 tapestry needle
Tapestry wools in the colours given in the key
45 cm (18 in) square cushion pad
Either 1m (1 yd) of velvet in a matching shade,
   30 cm (12 in) zip fastening to match, and
   1.6 m (1¾ yd) of piping cord
or finishing kit in ultramarine cotton velvet (for
   suppliers, see page 141)

Opposite: traditional 'Turkey rug' colours harmonize beautifully either with antique furnishings or with a modern ethnic-style decor. The cushion was stitched by Diane Chidzey.

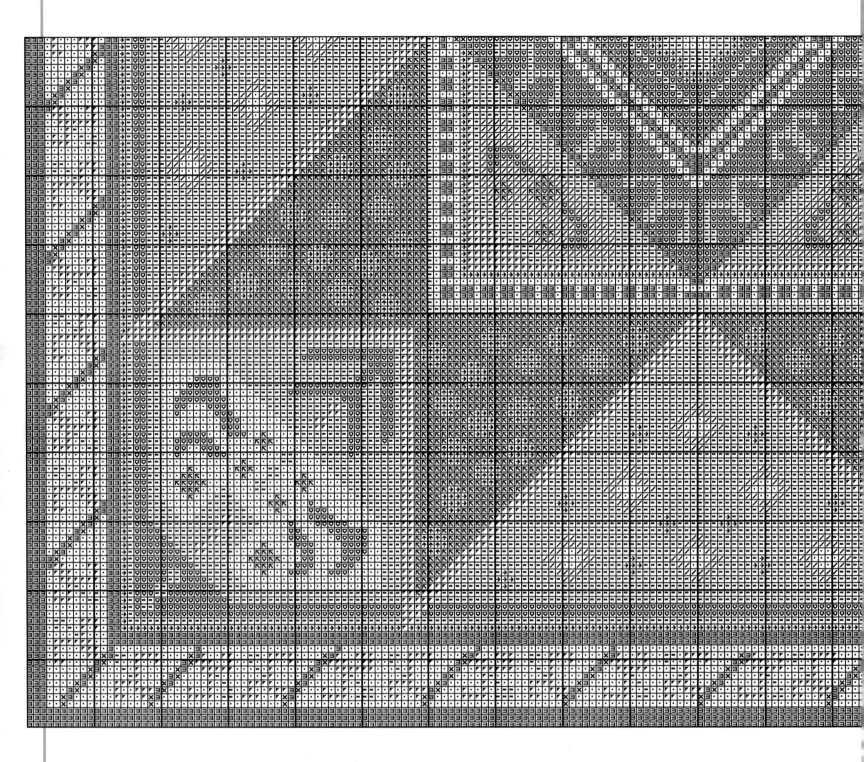

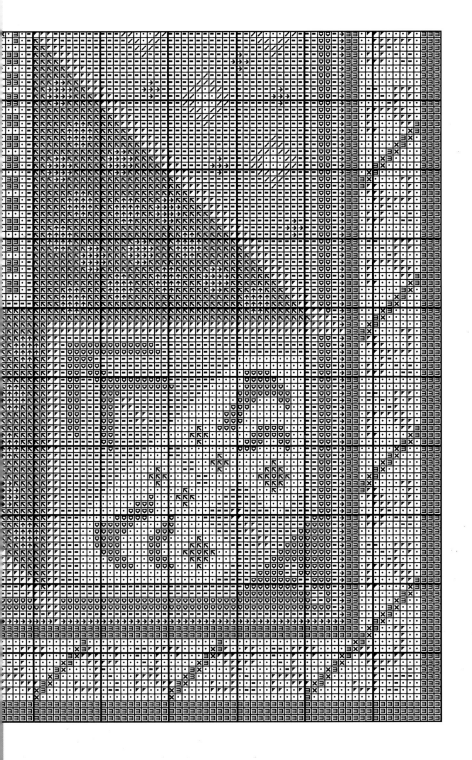

KURD CUSHION KEY

Paterna Persian yarn

- ▬ dark blue 510 (8 skeins) — 7 ✓
- • medium blue 511 (6 skeins) — 4½ + 3
- ╱ light blue 513 (1 skein) — 1 ✓
- ◩ red 840 (5 skeins) — 5 ✓
- → puce 910 (3 skeins) — 3 ✓
- ↑ dark pink 901 (1 skein) — 1 ✓
- ✕ cream 734 (1 skein) — ✓
- ◩ gold 731 (3 skeins) ✓
- ▽ green 642 (3 skeins) ✓
- ☰ charcoal 221 (4 skeins)

INSTRUCTIONS

1 Every tenth line on the chart is heavier than the other lines on the grid (equivalent to every tenth line of holes of your canvas). If you are uncertain about working from the chart, you could mark every tenth line of holes of your canvas each way, using a waterproof (permanent) marker, so that the marks will not run and damage your finished embroidery.

2 Prepare and frame your canvas in the usual way, then start from the centre and stitch the design from the chart, using continental tent stitch. If you are using Paterna yarn you will only need 2 strands of wool in your needle.

3 When you have stitched the whole design, either stretch (see page 140) or press the embroidery on the back with a hot steam iron over a damp cloth and gently pull back into shape.

4 Trim the canvas edges to leave a 12 mm (½ in) allowance of unworked canvas around the embroidery, then make the cushion cover, either using a prepared kit or as shown overleaf.

PREPARING COVERED PIPING

1 First prepare bias strips of your chosen fabric to cover the cord. The bias strips should be sufficiently wide to wrap around the cord and leave 12 mm (½ in) seam allowances. To prepare the strips, take a 1 m (1 yd) square of fabric and fold diagonally in half to find the bias. Using chalk or a fabric marker, mark the back of the fabric with sufficient strips to cover the cord.

2 Cut and join strips (at the same time, prepare pieces for the front framework and for the back of the cushion, see below), then pin and baste the fabric over the piping cord. Stitch the fabric in place, stitching close to the cord.

MAKING THE CUSHION COVER

The cover described here has a 30 cm (12 in) zip fastening in the back. The needlepoint has been framed with velvet strips.

1 Trim the embroidery to leave a 12 mm (½ in) allowance all around. Cut four strips from the backing fabric, each 45 cm (18 in) long (the size of the finished cover, plus two 12 mm/½ in seam allowances), and 6.2 cm (2½ in) wide (the width of the finished framework, plus 12 mm/½ in seam allowances). If you are using velvet, cut two strips across the fabric and two lengthways, then stitch them together so that the nap lies in one direction on the finished cover.

2 Leaving an even amount of spare fabric at each end, attach the strips one by one to the sides of the needlepoint, starting and finishing at embroidered corners. Mitre the strips together at adjoining corners, so that the embroidery is set in a mitred framework of velvet.

3 Also from the backing fabric, cut two pieces, both to the width of the front cover (including seam allowances). Cut one piece two thirds the depth of the cover, plus one 12 mm (½ in) seam allowance and one 2.5 cm (1 in) seam allowance (the seam allowance at the top or bottom edge of the cover and the seam allowance for the zip fastening). Cut the second piece one third the depth of the back, plus seam allowances.

4 Baste the two pieces together. Leaving a gap at the centre for the zip fastening and taking a 2.5 cm (1 in) seam allowance, join the two pieces at each end of the basted seam. Press the seam open then stitch the zip in the usual way.

5 Pin, baste and stitch prepared, covered piping around the right side of the front (embroidered) cushion cover piece, starting and finishing about two thirds of the way down one side edge (see step 6, below). Match seam allowances and bring the piping around the corners in a gentle curve, clipping into the seam allowances where necessary.

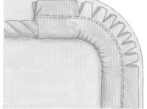

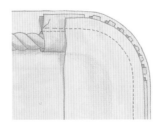

6 To join the ends of the piping together, first overlap them by about 2.5 cm (1 in). Unpick the two cut ends of bias to reveal the cord. Join the bias strip as shown. Trim and press the seam open. Unravel and splice the two ends of the cord, fold the bias strip over it, and finish basting around the edge.

7 With right sides together, lay the cushion back over the piped front section. It is important to make sure that the zip is open, so that the cover can be turned right side out when finished. Pin, baste and stitch the front and back covers together.

8 Trim across corners to reduce bulk. It may also help to trim the finished seam allowances to different widths to make them unobtrusive. Turn the finished cover right side out, insert the cushion pad, and close the fastening.

CRAZY CATS FOOTSTOOL

KELLY FLETCHER

ESIGNING THIS 'CRAZY CATS' FOOTSTOOL HAS TURNED ME INTO A FOOTSTOOL FANATIC, DOODLING NEW DESIGN IDEAS TO FIT WITHIN LARGE CIRCLES! FROM PAST EXPERIENCE I KNOW SOME OF THE DIFFICULTIES INVOLVED IN DESIGNING WITH CATS, THE MAIN ONE BEING THAT THEY ARE SUCH POPULAR SUBJECTS THAT IT IS A REAL CHALLENGE TO COME UP WITH ANYTHING NEW. I'VE THEREFORE TRIED TO TREAT MY CATS IN A SLIGHTLY WHIMSICAL MANNER, AND IN THIS FOOTSTOOL I'VE SIMPLIFIED THE CATS' SILHOUETTES SO THAT THE FLYING FELINES BECOME PURE PATTERN.

FINISHED SIZE

36 cm (14 in) in diameter

MATERIALS

48 cm (19 in) square of 10-gauge double-thread
 canvas
No 18 tapestry needle
Tapestry wools in the colours given in the key
Footstool, 37.5 cm (15 in) in diameter (for suppliers,
 see page 141)
Staple gun and staples

Opposite: you don't need to be a cat lover to feel inspired to stitch this footstool cover - I hope you enjoy it as much as I do!

STITCHING

1. Decide which part of the chart you would like to begin with. It's a good idea to start somewhere near the centre. Find the corresponding place on your blank canvas (the centre of your canvas corresponds with the centre of the chart).

2. Thread your needle with wool no longer than 40 cm (16 in). Following the chart as set out in the diagram, complete the design in half cross stitch. Each square on the chart represents one stitch on the canvas.

3. At this point I would normally recommend stretching the canvas, but I don't think it's necessary for this design, assuming that you are making it up into a footstool. The canvas gets pulled taut over the footstool cushion, and this was certainly all the stretching that my stitched canvas needed.

4. If you want to make a circular cushion and your canvas is at all distorted, then I suggest stretching it to form a good circle: press the embroidery on the back with a hot steam iron over a damp cloth and gently pull back into shape (for obvious reasons, leave the edges square until you are satisfied with the shape).

5. Finishing the footstool couldn't be simpler! Start by trimming the canvas to about 5 cm (2 in) all round the design.

6. Remove the cushion pad from the footstool and position the needlepoint over it - it takes a few attempts to get it exactly right.

7. Staple through the unstitched canvas to secure the needlepoint. Replace the cushion pad into the footstool, and it's all done!

CRAZY CATS KEY

Anchor Tapisserie wool

↓ palest maize 8032 (2 skeins)

T pale autumn gold 8054 (2 skeins)

— pale yellow orange 8114 (1 skein)

• light raspberry 8416 (6 skeins)

V raspberry 8418 (1 skein)

II damson 8510 (2 skeins)

Y palest steel grey 8712 (1 skein)

Z palest grass green 9162 (3 skeins)

I light beige brown 9636 (2 skeins)

3 granite 9774 (1 skein)

X grey 9794 (2 skeins)

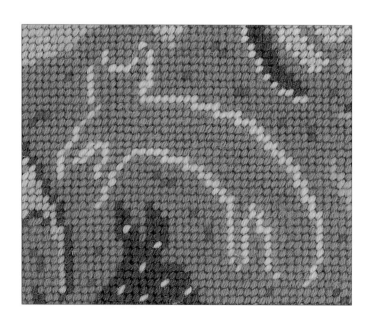

FUN FOR THE NURSERY

It is always a joy to make something for a child, and here are three needlepoint designs that will be certain to find favour – a colourful picture for a nursery wall, a pencil case that any child will love to take to school, and an intriguing ethnic cushion with a train of camels to fire the imagination!

ANIMAL NUMBERS PICTURE

KELLY FLETCHER

~

A NIMAL NUMBERS PICTURE IS A COLLECTION OF COLOURFUL ANIMALS, WITH A FLOWER FOR GOOD MEASURE. I'VE MADE MY DESIGN INTO A PICTURE BUT IT WOULD LOOK JUST AS GOOD AS A CUSHION. TO AVOID THE UNIFORMITY OF PATCHWORK SQUARES, I'VE OUTLINED EACH OF THE CORNER ANIMALS IN GREY, AND I'VE BOXED IN THE OTHER CHARACTERS. THE NUMBERS HAVE BEEN INCLUDED TO ADD AN EXTRA DIMENSION TO THE DESIGN. THERE'S PATTERN EVERYWHERE TOO: EACH EDGE OF THE BORDER IS DIFFERENT, AND THE ANIMALS AND PATCHES ARE SET AGAINST A PALE CHEQUERED BACKGROUND.

FINISHED SIZE

30 cm (12 in) square

MATERIALS

40 cm (16 in) square of 10-gauge double-thread
   canvas
No 18 tapestry needle
Tapestry wool in the colours given in the key
Frame – choose colours for the mount and frame
   which best suit your decor (I chose pale pink for
   the mount and grey blue for the frame, but there
   are endless combinations that would work well)

*Opposite: this is one design
you certainly will not tire of
while stitching, and the end
result is guaranteed to be a
great present for any child.*

INSTRUCTIONS

1 Decide which part of the chart you would
like to begin with. It's a good idea to start
somewhere near the centre. Find the
corresponding place on your blank canvas
(the centre of your canvas corresponds
with the centre of the chart).

2 Thread your needle with wool no longer
than 40 cm (16 in) – do not be tempted to
cut the lengths longer than this or it will
become very thin while working.
Following the chart as set out in the
diagram, complete the design, using half
cross stitch. Each square on the chart
represents one stitch on the canvas.

3 When the design is completed, stretch the
canvas if it has become distorted during
stitching. If you intend making the design
up into a picture it is essential to have
straight edges, and right angles at the
corners.

4 Unless you have experience of frame-
making or can enlist the help of someone
who does, I would recommend getting
your finished needlepoint framed by a
professional framer, who will also be happy
to help you with your choice of mount or
frame.

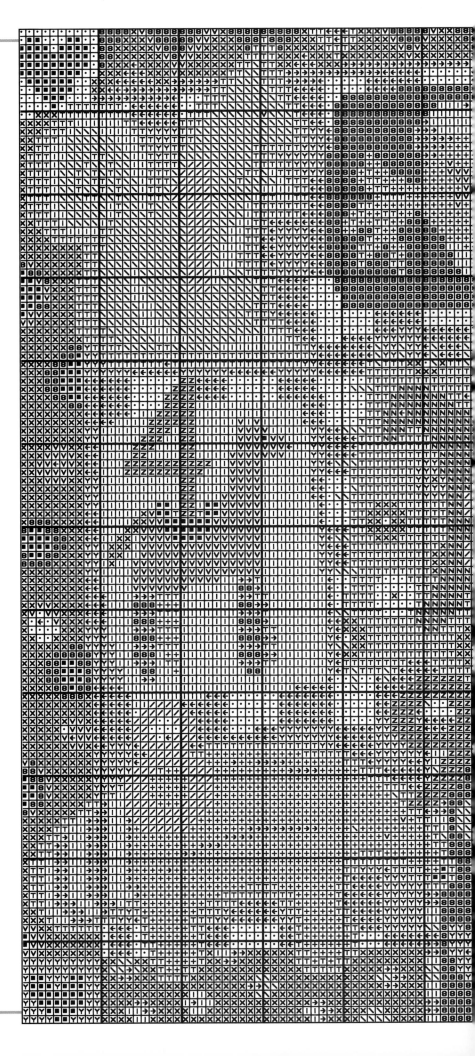

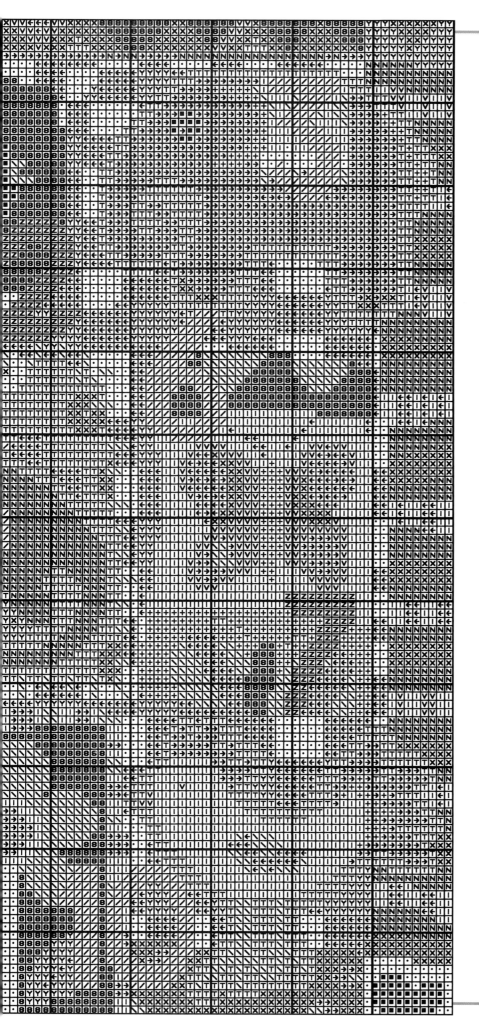

Anchor Tapisserie wool

←	white 8000 (3 skeins)
I	pale old gold 8114 (3 skeins)
\	palest tangerine 8152 (2 skeins)
+	palest rose pink 8392 (2 skeins)
→	cyclamen 8438 (2 skeins)
N	palest fuchsia 8452 (3 skeins)
X	pale lilac 8586 (2 skeins)
Z	dark periwinkle 8612 (1 skein)
8	pale cornflower blue 8684 (2 skeins)
V	cornflower blue 8690 (1 skein)
■	cloud grey 8704 (1 skein)
T	steel grey 8716 (3 skeins)
/	dark aqua 8938 (1 skein)
•	palest apple green 9092 (2 skeins)
Y	palest leaf green 9192 (2 skeins)

CAMEL CUSHION

MARCIA PARKINSON

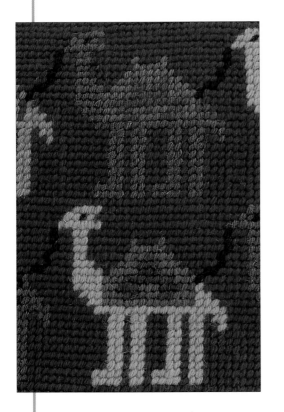

I FIRST GOT THE IDEA FOR A DESIGN SHOWING CAMELS WHILE VISITING A MAGICAL PLACE CALLED TINFOU, AN OASIS VILLAGE SITUATED IN THE SOUTH-EASTERN REGION OF MOROCCO JUST BEFORE THE SAHARA DEVELOPS INTO AN AREA OF SAND DUNES. THE COLOURS I HAVE CHOSEN REMIND ME OF THIS PART OF THE WORLD, BUT THE PATTERN IS BASED ON A VERY OLD DESIGN ORIGINATING IN THE BARDA DISTRICT OF AZERBAJAN IN THE RUSSIAN CAUCASUS.

FINISHED SIZE

50 cm (20 in) square approximately

MATERIALS

75 cm (30 in) of double-thread rug canvas, 90 cm
 (1 yd) wide
Large-eyed needle
Six-fold whipping wool for rugs by Readicut
55 cm (22 in) square of sturdy backing fabric - the
 fabric chosen should be similar in weight to the
 needlework. Anything lighter will wear out more
 quickly and will not be strong enough to support
 the worked piece. A plain linen union or lightweight upholstery sail-cloth would be ideal.
Sewing thread
55 cm (22 in) square cushion pad

Opposite: this cushion, which will carry an imaginative child across the world, has been trimmed with a heavy twisted cord with tasselled corners, which carry through the nomadic theme. The embroidery was stitched by Lynn Waude.

INSTRUCTIONS

1 Work pattern from the chart, using half cross stitch and making sure that the design is centred on the canvas. When the stitching is completed, stretch the finished work to bring it back to a true square.

2 Press the backing fabric. Centring the fabric over the stitched canvas, baste the right side of the fabric to the right side of the needlework. Stitch around the edge of the needlework, leaving a 30 cm (12 in) gap along one side for turning. Make a second row of stitching just outside the first row to strengthen the seam.

3 Trim the canvas, leaving an allowance of about 4 cm (1½ in) excess all round. Trim diagonally across corners to within 2.5 cm (1 in) of stitching. Turn the needlework to the right side; insert the cushion pad and neatly slip-stitch the opening.

4 Using the remainder of the rust, cream and gold wools, make a 3-colour twisted cord, as shown overleaf.

5 Prepare the cord for the cushion. First, tie the two ends of the cord so that it forms a large ring and the knot is positioned to create a tassel with ends about 8 cm (3 in) long. Trim the ends of the tassel so that they are even.

6 Tie a second knot so that the distance between the two knots is 51 cm (20 in), again forming a tassel below the knot. Trim the ends as before, making the second tassel the same size at the first one. You now have a ring of cord with two tassels spaced 51 cm (20⅜ in) apart.

7 Slipstitch the tasselled section of the cord to the bottom edge of the cushion, making sure that the tassels sit on the corners.

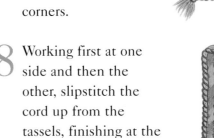

8 Working first at one side and then the other, slipstitch the cord up from the tassels, finishing at the top corners.

9 Twist the cord at each top corner to take up the slack and to form loops. Stitch these firmly and slipstitch the remaining cord along the top edge of the cushion.

MAKING A 3-COLOUR CORD

1 Knot the ends of the three colours together and persuade someone to hold the knotted end for you. (If you have no-one to hold the knot for you, hook it over a coat hook or door handle.)

2 Holding them taut, feed out the strands of wool to their full length (if they are of unequal length, trim them to measure the same), then tie the other ends together.

3 Put a pen or ruler through the knotted end you are holding and turn it to twist the wool. Keep turning until the wool is tightly twisted along its full length.

4 Take the end you are holding and give it to the person at the other end, so that they have hold of both ends. Without the wool becoming entangled, hold the twisted threads in the middle and shake so that they twist together into a cord. Tie a knot in the end. This should give you a 6-stranded cord.

5 Repeat the process, twisting the cord and folding it in half again to produce a 12-stranded cord.

6 Tie off the loose end to stop the cord unravelling. This should give you sufficient cord to go round the edge of the cushion cover.

CAMEL CUSHION KEY

Readicut rug wools

▬	rust 70 (3 balls)
•	gold 3 (2 balls)
/	wine 60 (1 ball)
↖	pink 93 (1 ball)
→	light green 17 (1 ball)
↑	dark green 96 (1 ball)
✕	blue 74 (1 ball)
▪▪	turquoise 45 (1 ball)
▽	cream 2 (1 ball)
⊒	fawn 87 (1 ball)
◤	grey 50 (1 ball)

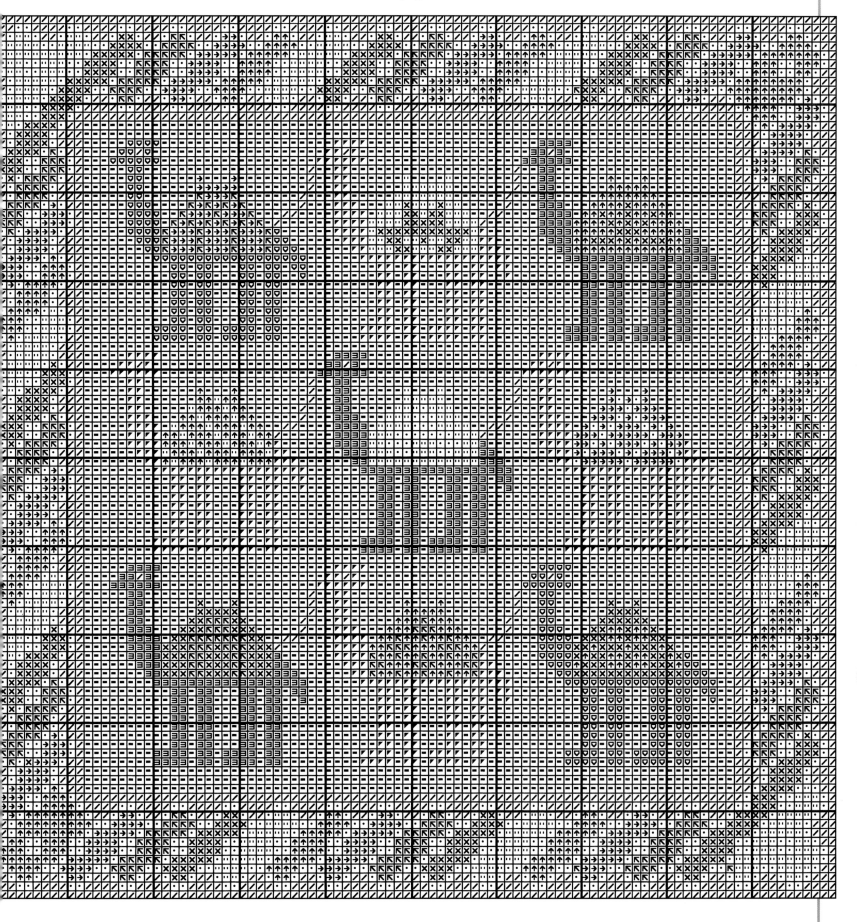

TIGER PENCIL CASE

KELLY FLETCHER

J UNGLE ANIMALS ARE VERY POPULAR WITH MY FIVE-YEAR-OLD SON AND HIS FRIENDS, AND I'M SURE THIS CHEERY TIGER WILL HAVE PLENTY OF ADMIRERS. PART OF THE APPEAL OF A SMALL PROJECT SUCH AS A PENCIL CASE IS THE SPEED AT WHICH IT CAN BE MADE, SO I WOULD DEFINITELY RECOMMEND ADDING A FABRIC BACKING TO THE PENCIL CASE RATHER THAN STITCHING THE TIGER TWICE. I BACKED MINE WITH A BRIGHT YELLOW FABRIC AND INSERTED A RED ZIP TO BRING OUT SOME OF THE COLOURS USED IN THE DESIGN.

FINISHED SIZE

10 x 20 cm (4 x 8 in)

MATERIALS

20 x 30 cm (8 x 12 in) of 10-gauge double-thread
  canvas
No 18 tapestry needle
Tapestry wool in the colours given in the key
13 x 23 cm (5¼ x 11¼ in) of a suitable backing fabric
22.5 cm (9 in) square of lining fabric
20 cm (8 in) zip fastener

Opposite: this quick and easy design makes an unusual gift for a child; choose a sturdy lining fabric, so that coloured pencils will not push through and spoil the wool colours.

INSTRUCTIONS

1 Decide which part of the chart you would like to begin with. It's a good idea to start somewhere near the centre. Find the corresponding place on your blank canvas (the centre of your canvas corresponds with the centre of the chart).

2 Thread your needle with wool no longer than 40 cm (16 in) – do not be tempted to cut the lengths longer than this or it will become very thin while working. Following the chart as set out in the diagram, complete the design, using half cross stitch. Each square on the chart represents one stitch on the canvas.

3 When the design is completed, stretch the canvas if it has become distorted during stitching. Once it has dried, you can continue with the making-up process.

4 Trim the canvas to leave 1.5 cm (⅝ in) all round the edge of the finished needlepoint.

5 Fold under and baste the 1.5 cm (⅝ in) seam allowance along one edge of the backing fabric, and the unworked canvas along the top edge of the embroidery. With the right sides of the fabric and the right side of the zip upwards, baste the zip in place between the two folded edges, then machine stitch, using the zipper foot of your machine.

6 Open the zip. With wrong sides together, and taking a 1.5 cm (⅝ in) seam allowance, stitch the bottom and side edges of the front and backing fabric together. Trim away excess fabric at the corners, then turn the pencil case right side out.

7 Fold the lining fabric in half, right sides together, and stitch the side edges, taking a 12 mm (½ in) seam allowance.

8 Fold back the remaining edges and fit the lining pocket snugly inside the pencil case. Hand stitch the lining to the inside of the zip opening, and anchor it in place at the bottom corners with a few small stitches.

TIGER PENCIL CASE KEY

Anchor Tapisserie wool

■	pale maize 8034 (1 skein)	K	pale purple 8524 (1 skein)
II	pale yellow orange 8114 (1 skein)	Z	cornflower blue 8688 (1 skein)
—	deep flame red 8202 (2 skeins)	O	peacock green 8918 (1 skein)
3	pale cherry red 8212 (1 skein)	V	palest grass green 9162 (1 skein)
Y	palest rose pink 8392 (1 skein)	I	mink 9680 (1 skein)

DINE IN ELEGANCE

Presentation makes food taste all the better, and touches of hand-stitchery help to create a relaxing and comfortable ambience for enjoyable meals with your friends and family. The smaller items, such as the mat or the tea cosy, would also make very charming gifts.

PRIMROSES CHAIR SEAT

STELLA EDWARDS

RIMROSES ARE A CHEERFUL SIGN IN THE GARDEN THAT WINTER IS COMING TO AN END. THEIR DELICATE LITTLE FLOWERS ARE ALWAYS THOUGHT OF AS BEING YELLOW, BUT WHEN YOU START LOOKING AT THEM THERE ARE LOTS OF DIFFERENT SHADES OF YELLOWS, CREAMS AND EVEN PALE ORANGE, GIVING THEM A WONDERFUL DEPTH OF COLOUR. I HAVE EXAGGERATED THE COLOURS AS I FELT VERY SUBTLE TONES WOULD NOT BE STRONG ENOUGH.

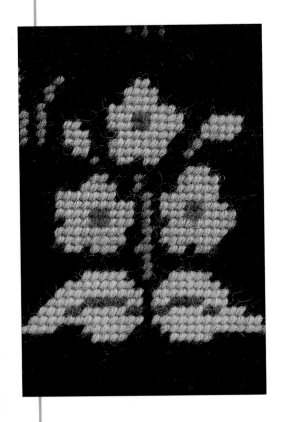

FINISHED SIZE

51 cm (20 in) front, narrowing to 38 cm (15 in) at the back; 53 cm (21 in) down the sides, approximately

MATERIALS

60 x 57.5 cm (24 x 23 in) of 10-gauge double-thread canvas
No 20 tapestry needle
Tapestry wool in the colours given in the key
Dining chair*
Upholstery pins
Strong thread and large-eyed needle
Backing fabric
Staples and stapler

Note: the size of the finished cover can easily be adjusted by adding or omitting primrose clumps.*

Opposite: dining chairs with hand-embroidered seats look both comfortable and elegant, and needlepoint is an extremely hard-wearing upholstery fabric.

INSTRUCTIONS

1 Follow the chart to work the design, using half cross stitch throughout. Starting in the middle (the middle of the chart should correspond with the centre point of your canvas), embroider the primroses first, and then fill in the background. The symbols on the chart and in the key correspond with the wool numbers.

2 After completing the embroidery, press the back with a hot steam iron over a damp cloth and gently pull back into shape.

3 Trim around the edges of the finished needlepoint, cutting across the corners at an angle.

4 Carefully position the embroidery over the chair seat and pin it in place.

5 Lace the canvas edges together on the back with long stitches, working firstly from side to side and then top to bottom.

6 Cut backing fabric to cover the underside of the seat and conceal the lacing. Turn the edges under and then staple the backing fabric in place.

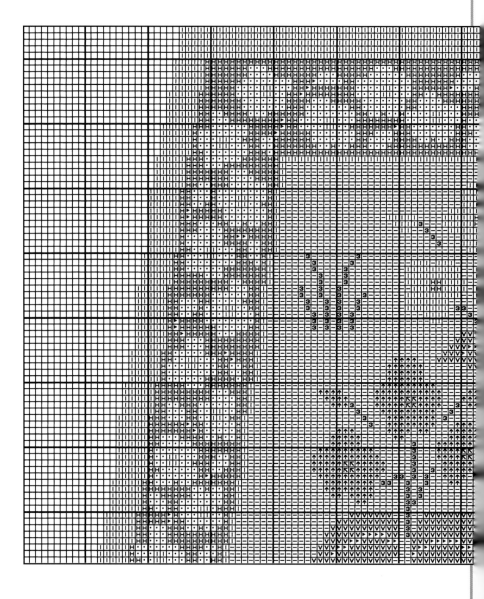

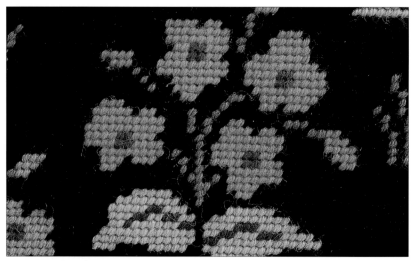

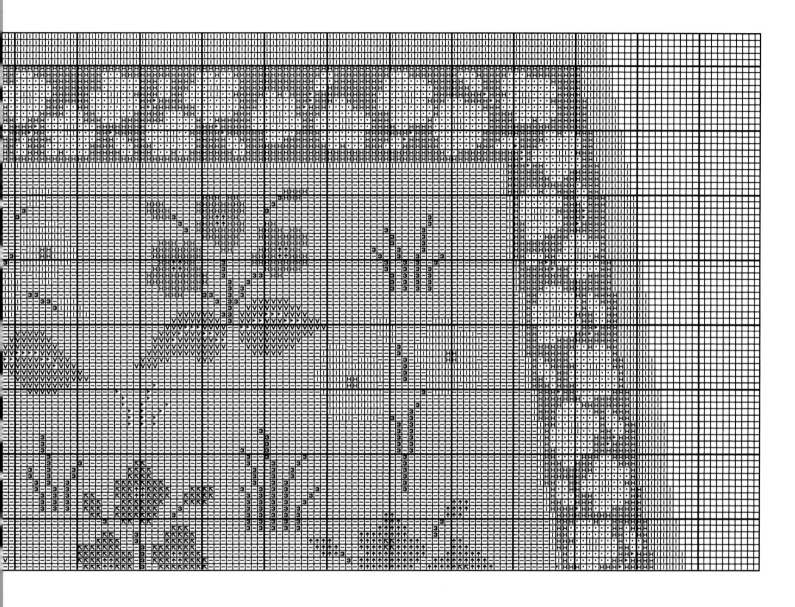

PRIMROSES CHAIR SEAT KEY

Anchor Tapisserie wool

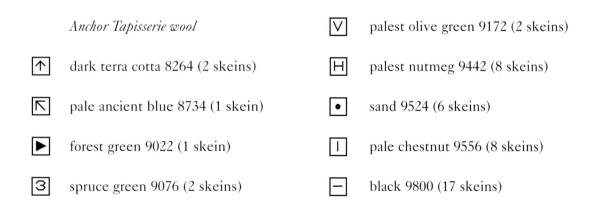

↑	dark terra cotta 8264 (2 skeins)	V	palest olive green 9172 (2 skeins)
↖	pale ancient blue 8734 (1 skein)	H	palest nutmeg 9442 (8 skeins)
▶	forest green 9022 (1 skein)	•	sand 9524 (6 skeins)
3	spruce green 9076 (2 skeins)	I	pale chestnut 9556 (8 skeins)
		—	black 9800 (17 skeins)

PRIMROSES CHAIR SEAT KEY

↑ dark terra cotta 8264

↖ pale ancient blue 8734

▶ forest green 9022

3 spruce green 9076

V palest olive green 9172

H palest nutmeg 9442

• sand 9524

I pale chestnut 9556

– black 9800

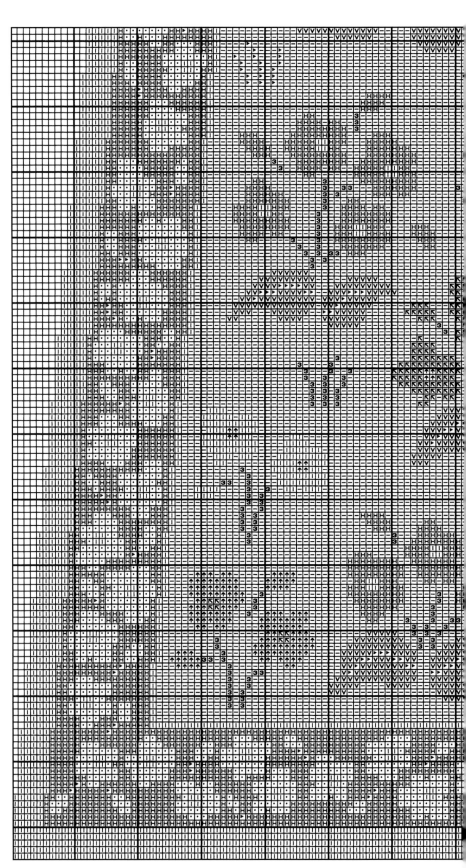

GRAPE VINE TABLE MAT

SANDRA HARDY

~

AN INHERITED ANTIQUE MIRROR WITH A FASCINATING FRAME OF INTERTWINING VINE LEAVES AND GRAPES HAS BEEN THE STARTING POINT FOR SEVERAL NEEDLEPOINT PROJECTS. THIS, TOGETHER WITH POOLE POTTERY'S DELIGHTFUL VINEYARD PATTERN, INSPIRED THIS PLACEMAT DESIGN. THE SPONGING ON THE CHINA HAS BEEN RECREATED BY USING A MIXED THREAD OF GREEN AND BLUE, INTERSPERSED WITH STITCHES IN CREAM, PLAIN BLUE AND GREEN. PLASTIC CANVAS WAS SELECTED BECAUSE IT IS WASHABLE AND RELATIVELY RIGID COMPARED TO ORDINARY CANVAS.

FINISHED SIZE

27.5 x 20.5 cm (11 x 8¼ in)

MATERIALS

27.5 x 20.5 cm (11 x 8¼ in) of 14-gauge clear-coloured plastic canvas (one sheet)
No 22 tapestry needle
Stranded cotton in the colours given in the key
30.5 x 23.5 cm (12¼ x 9½ in) of plain cotton backing fabric
Matching sewing thread

Opposite: this delicately-interwoven pattern has been stitched in washable stranded cottons on plastic canvas.

INSTRUCTIONS

1 Start and finish all threads as for normal canvas. Use six strands of cotton in the needle throughout, and lengths no longer than 40 cm (16 in), to prevent fraying.

2 All rows of stitching are finished using the last hole on the grid. The plastic beyond must be covered with an overcast stitch.

3 Mark the centre of the canvas with a waterproof pen, and start stitching the stalks and leaves first, then follow on with the grapes. Where two colours are given beside a symbol, use three strands of each shade.

4 Take care when stitching to keep a medium tension, as stitches which are very tight will cause the mat to curl and distort, so that it no longer lies flat.

5 When you have finished the vines, stitch the blue and green 'sponging', and finally the plain background.

6 Where there are several colour changes close to one another, try to avoid a build-up of thread in a particular place on the reverse side of the canvas, as this could prevent the mat from lying flat.

7 The overcasting stitch on the outside edges completes the stitching.

8 Fold in a 1.5 cm (⅝ in) allowance on all sides of the backing fabric and carefully pin it to the wrong side of the mat. Slipstitch the backing to the underside of the overcasting edge stitches.

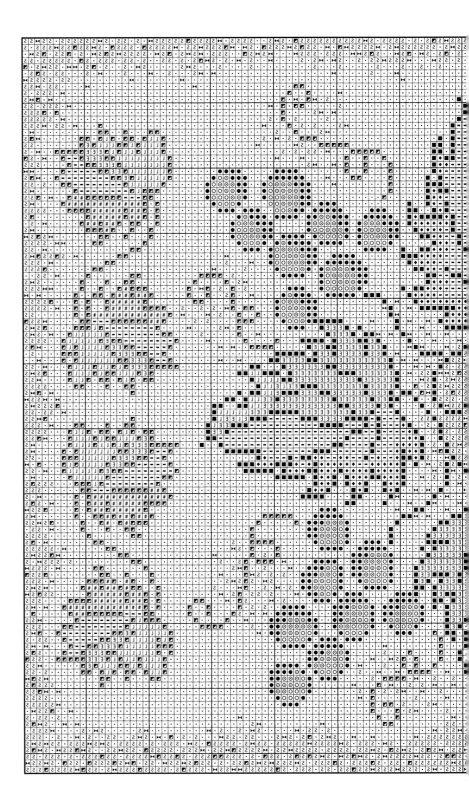

GRAPE VINE TABLE MAT KEY

DMC Stranded Cotton

- ● navy blue 336 (1 skein)
- ■ dark green 367 (1 skein)
- ⊔ yellow green 369 (13 skeins)
- ▷◁ mid-blue 793 (1 skein)
- ◯ light blue 794 (3 skeins)
- # light green 966 (3 skeins)
- ◉ dark blue 3807 (1 skein)
- ◩ mid-green 320 (3 skeins)
- · cream 746 (3 skeins)
- ▬ light mid-green 368 (3 skeins) and light green
- Ǝ light mid-green and yellow green
- ◆ light mid-green and mid-green
- S light blue and yellow green

Where 2 colours are combined, use 3 strands of each colour

TEACUP CUPBOARD

SANDRA HARDY

~

A GLASS CABINET FULL OF ASSORTED CHINA TEACUPS IS A CHILDHOOD MEMORY FROM VISITS TO MY GRANDMOTHER. THIS, TOGETHER WITH CHESHIRE DISTRIBUTION'S FURNISHING FABRIC 'TEACUPS', AND A CONSUMING PASSION FOR DRINKING TEA, INPIRED THIS DESIGN. AN ANTIQUE-COLOURED CANVAS HAS BEEN USED HERE, SO THAT THE TINY SPECKS OF BROWN SHOWING THROUGH GIVE THE CUP AN AUTHENTICALLY AGED LOOK!

FINISHED SIZE

15.2 cm (6 in) square

MATERIALS

25 cm (10 in) square of 12-gauge antique-coloured
   canvas
No 18 tapestry needle
Tapestry wool in the colours given in the key
15.2 cm (6 in) square of cardboard/mount card
15.2 cm (6 in) square of lightweight polyester
   wadding
Crochet cotton
Large-eyed needle
Adhesive pads or double-sided tape
Key cupboard with an aperture in the door 15.2 cm
   (6 in) square (for suppliers, see page 141)

Opposite: designed for keys, this small cupboard is also an ideal size to store salt and pepper pots.

INSTRUCTIONS

1. Mark the centre of the canvas and set it in a frame. Start by stitching the yellow cup rim and border edge, using half cross stitch and making sure that the centre mark of your canvas corresponds with the centre of the chart.

2. Stitch the coloured border on the cup, together with the floral corner patterns.

3. Gradually fill in the cup and handle with the ecru and grey.

4. Finally stitch the background stripes, ensuring that the central one is in the correct position.

5. Remove the canvas from the frame and lace it over the polyester wadding and cardboard mount.

6. Secure the design to the cupboard with adhesive pads or double-sided tape.

TEACUP CUPBOARD KEY

DMC Tapestry yarn

■	dark grey 7275 (1 skein)
◆	dark yellow 7474 (1 skein)
2	light grey 7510 (1 skein)
8	brown 7520 (1 skein)
◧	dark green 7542 (1 skein)
▲	medium yellow 7725 (1 skein)
⎿	light yellow 7727 (1 skein)
♡	medium pink 7762 (1 skein)
★	dark blue 7798 (1 skein)
✕	light blue 7799 (1 skein)
♥	dark pink 7851 (1 skein)
Z	light green 7954 (1 skein)
▪	ecru (2 skeins)
O	light pink 7179 (2 skeins)
◹	very light yellow 7905 (2 skeins)

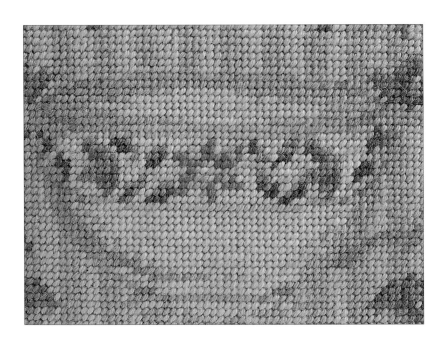

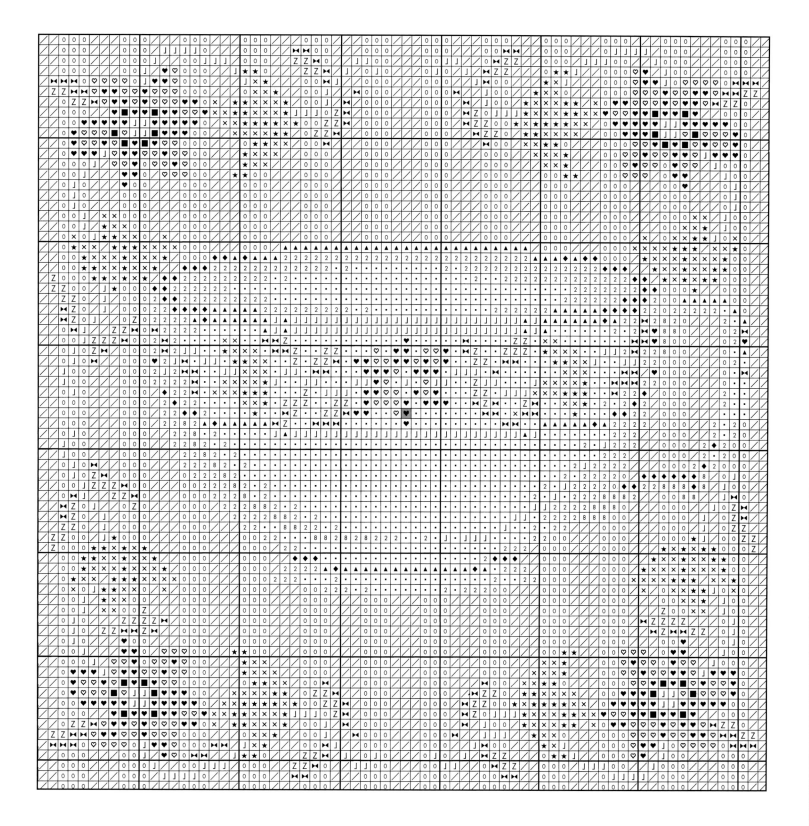

IRISES AND POPPIES COSY

STELLA EDWARDS

THE GLOWING RED OF THE POPPY IS NO LONGER A COMMON SIGHT, BUT FOR THOUSANDS OF YEARS CORN AND POPPY AND CIVILIZATION HAVE GONE TOGETHER. POPPIES AFTER A BATTLE SEEMED A NATURAL CONSEQUENCE IN MORE THAN ONE EUROPEAN WAR, THE FRAGILE BLOOD-RED FLOWER BECOMING SYMBOLIC OF LIFE LOST. THE IRIS, ON THE OTHER HAND, AND ESPECIALLY THE BEAUTIFUL ORCHID-LIKE BLOOMS OF THE WILD SPECIES, THE YELLOW FLAG, HAD A REPUTATION FOR ROMANCE AND HAD BECOME A POET'S PLANT BY THE 19TH CENTURY.

FINISHED SIZE

33 x 38 cm (13 x 15 in) maximum height and width

MATERIALS

40 x 50 cm (16 x 20 in) of 10-gauge double-thread canvas

Tapestry wool in the colours given in the key

No 20 tapestry needle

40 cm (16 in) square of backing fabric

2 x 40 cm (16 in) squares of polyester wadding

4 x 40 cm (16 in) squares of lining fabric, to cover the wadding

70 cm (¾ yd) of decorative upholstery cord

Opposite: this is a bright, summery design with lots of colours, which will match any tea service. Although just embroidered on one side here, the design could be repeated on the back of the cosy.

INSTRUCTIONS

1 Following the chart, stitch the design, starting in the middle. Use half cross-stitch throughout and stitch the flowers and leaves first and then the background.

2 Press the embroidery on the back with a hot steam iron over a damp cloth and gently pull back into shape.

3 Trim any excess canvas to within 12 mm (½ in) of the embroidery.

4 Cut out four pieces of lining fabric to the same size as the embroidery and two pieces of wadding, cutting the curved edge to the same size, but trimming 1.5 cm (⅝ in) from the bottom edge.

5 Make a 6 mm (¼ in) turning along one edge of the backing fabric and, with right sides facing, pin and stitch the embroidery to the backing fabric. Match the folded edge of the backing to the bottom edge of the canvas, but leave the bottom edges open. When you have stitched the backing to the embroidery, trim the backing fabric so that the curved edges of the backing and needlepoint match.

6 Carefully turn up the canvas and backing fabric around the bottom edge; hem the backing fabric and catchstitch the canvas turning to the back of the embroidery.

7 Sew a wadding section to the wrong side of a lining section, taking a 1.5 cm (⅝ in) seam allowance and stitching all around the curved edge only. Repeat with the second wadding section. Trim the wadding close to the seamline, to reduce bulk.

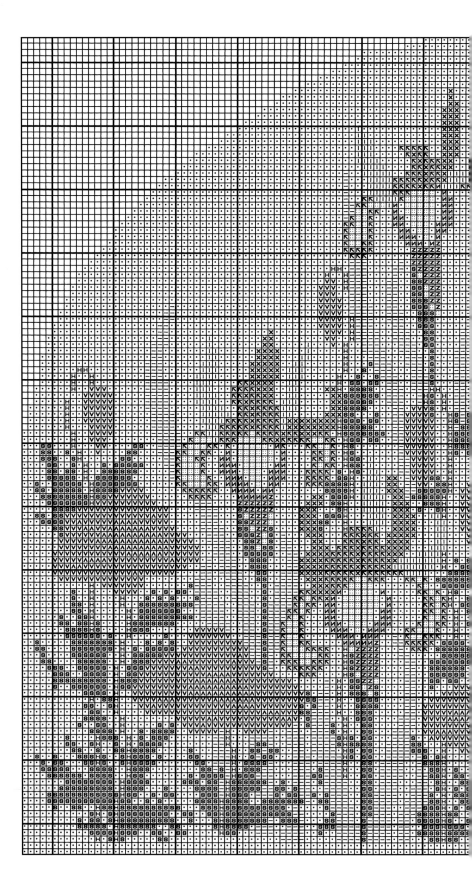

8 Take one of the remaining lining sections and place it on a wadded piece (with the linings right sides together). Stitch all around, leaving a gap at the bottom edge for turning. Turn the piece right side out and sew up the gap. Repeat. Neatly stitch the two pieces together around the curved seam, and insert into the tea cosy.

IRISES AND POPPIES COSY

Anchor Tapisserie wool

●	pale maize 8036 (4 skeins)
∷	pale yellow orange 8114 (1 skein)
V	deep flame red 8202 (2 skeins)
X	cornflower blue 8690 (1 skein)
K	lilac 8590 (1 skein)
I	deep lilac 8592 (1 skein)
И	palest periwinkle 8602 (1 skein)
H	laurel 9006 (1 skein)
S	apple green 9100 (2 skeins)
—	dark apple green 9120 (2 skeins)
Z	palest parrot green 9152 (1 skein)
Λ	black 9800 (1 skein)

GARDENING DELIGHTS

Here are three ideas for those who enjoy dining or relaxing outdoors in comfort and style. The foxglove cushion would be ideal for a conservatory; the table setting would add to the elegance of an outdoor lunch, and for keen gardeners there is a charming book cover.

FOXGLOVE CUSHION

STELLA EDWARDS

F OXGLOVES ARE A WONDERFUL SIGHT ALONG THE BANKS OF COUNTRY LANES AND ARE ALWAYS SURROUNDED BY BEES, WHICH I HAVE TRIED TO CAPTURE IN THIS DESIGN. THE VIBRANT PINKS AND PURPLES OF THE FLOWERS SIT WONDERFULLY AGAINST THE DARK GREEN, WHICH IS ALSO THE PERFECT BACKGROUND FOR THE LITTLE BEES. APART FROM THEIR STRIKING AND HIGHLY ORNAMENTAL APPEARANCE, FOXGLOVES WERE KNOWN TO COUNTRY FOLK TO BE BOTH POISONOUS AND – IN SMALL DOSES – MEDICINAL, LONG BEFORE DOCTORS DISCOVERED THEM AS THE SOURCE OF THE DRUG DIGITALIN.

FINISHED SIZE

38 x 30 cm (15 x 12 in)

MATERIALS

50 x 40 cm (20 x 16 in) of 10-gauge double-thread
  canvas
No 20 tapestry needle
40 x 32.5 cm (16 x 13 in) of a suitable backing fabric
40 x 32.5 cm (16 x 13 in) cushion pad, for a well
  filled effect
1.5 m (1¾ yd) of decorative upholstery cord
Tapestry wool in the colours given in the key

Opposite: the foxglove design conjures up heady days of summer with its exuberant colours and humming bees.

INSTRUCTIONS

1 Find the centre of the canvas. Start stitching the design from the middle, following the chart. Use half cross stitch throughout. Choose the correct colours of wool by referring to the symbols on the chart and in the key.

2 Remove the finished embroidery from the frame. Press it on the back with a hot steam iron over a damp cloth and gently pull back into shape.

3 Keeping the embroidery centred, trim the canvas edges to make the embroidery the same size as the backing fabric.

4 With right sides facing, sew the embroidery to the backing fabric, starting one third along the bottom edge and sewing around the four corners. Leave a gap about 15 cm (6 in) long.

5 Trim back any excess canvas and fabric, cutting the corners at an angle to reduce bulk.

6 Turn the work right sides out.

7 Insert the cushion pad and neatly slipstitch across the gap, leaving a small opening for the cord ends.

8 Stitch the cord around the edges of the cushion, tucking the ends inside the opening and securing them.

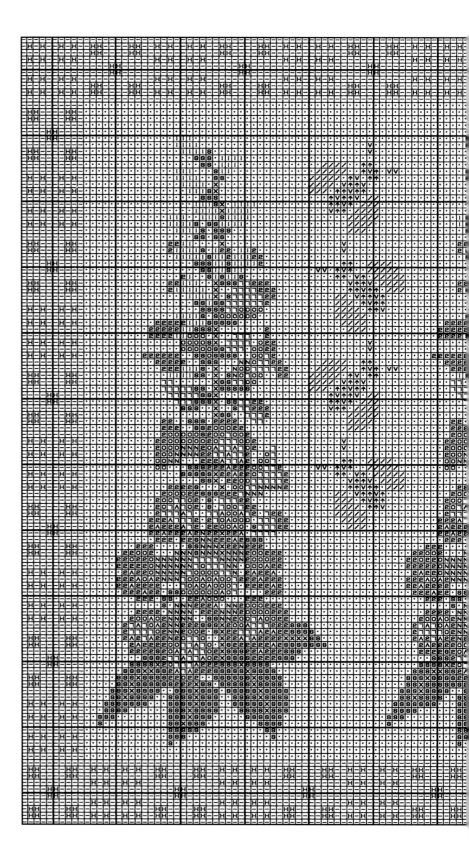

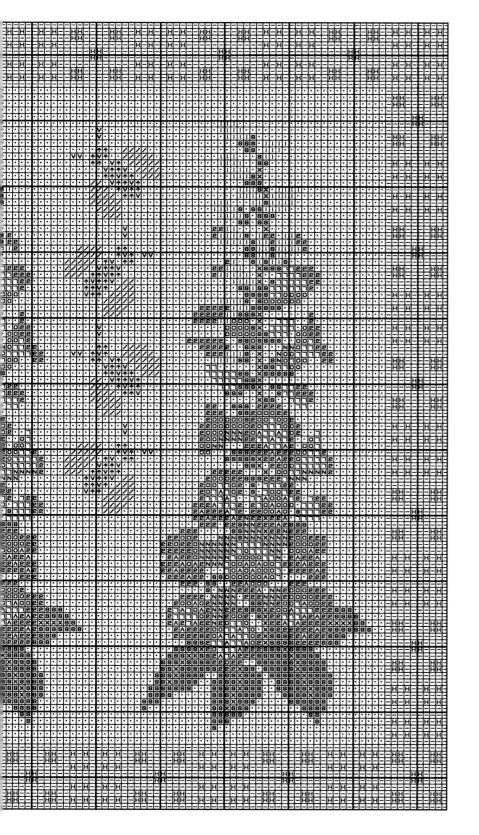

FOXGLOVE CUSHION KEY

Anchor Tapisserie wool

↑   light yellow orange 8114 (1 skein)

2   light cyclamen 8434 (2 skeins)

⌐   magenta 8488 (2 skeins)

O   deep magenta 8490 (2 skeins)

N   purple 8526 (2 skeins)

∧   deep purple 8528 (1 skein)

—   cathedral blue 8786 (2 skeins)

H   deep cathedral blue 8790 (1 skein)

•   forest green 9022 (4 skeins)

I   light bright leaf 9094 (2 skeins)

S   apple green 9096 (2 skeins)

X   deep apple green 9100 (1 skein)

╱   pale grey 9786 (1 skein)

V   black 9800 (1 skein)

SUMMER FRUITS SETTING

CHRISTINA MARSH

~

THE OPTIMISM OF THE POST-WAR YEARS BROUGHT A WAVE OF MODERNISM, WHICH EMBRACED EVERY ASPECT OF LIFE. HOMES DISCARDED THE DRAB COLOURS AND SUBDUED DESIGNS OF THE WAR YEARS AND THESE WERE REPLACED WITH THE BRIGHT COLOURS AND BOLD PATTERNS EVOKED IN THIS SUMMERY TABLE MAT SETTING.

FINISHED SIZE

Table mat 27.5 x 33 cm (11 x 13 in)
Napkin ring 3.5 x 15 cm (1½ x 6 in)

MATERIALS

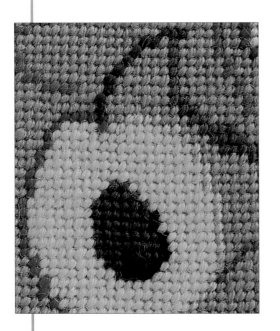

Table mat
38 x 43 cm (15 x 17 in) of 12-gauge mono interlock
   canvas
No 20 tapestry needle
Tapestry wool in the colours given in the key
30 cm x 35.5 cm (12 x 14 in) of medium-weight fabric
   for backing
Matching sewing cotton

Napkin ring
10 x 25 cm (4 x 10 in) 12-gauge mono interlock canvas
Needle and wool as above
33 cm (13 in) of blue bias binding, 12 mm (½ in) wide

Opposite: the rich variety of these fruit slices will add a splash of colour to your table and is an ideal design for informal and al fresco parties.

INSTRUCTIONS

1 Find the centre of the canvas by counting or by folding it in half, then half again and making a single stitch where the folds cross.

2 Mount the canvas in a tapestry frame, making sure it is evenly tensioned. Work the design in continental tent stitch, following the symbols on the chart and key. Start on one of the fruits closest to the centre; each fruit should be completely stitched before you start another.

3 When the design is complete, stitch the background, preferably working in diagonal rows (basketweave) as this will minimize distortion and make the stitching more even.

4 Remove the finished needlepoint from the frame and stretch the canvas back into shape if necessary.

5 To make table mat, cut away surplus canvas from the edges, leaving a 12 mm (½ in) border of unworked canvas. Place the canvas and the backing fabric together (right sides facing) and machine around three sides.

6 Trim diagonally across the corners; turn the work to the right side, and press with a damp cloth. Fold in the surplus material at the open side and neatly slipstitch to finish.

7 To make napkin ring, trim surplus canvas, leaving a 12 mm (½ in) border of unworked canvas round the embroidery. Pin one strip of bias binding to each edge of the longest side and machine. Place the two short edges together (right sides facing) and machine. Turn the bias binding to the back of the work and slipstitch to finish.

SUMMER FRUITS SETTING KEY

Anchor Tapisserie wool

•	white 8002 (3 skeins)
9	brown 8106 (1 skein)
—	yellow 8116 (3 skeins)
H	orange 8168 (3 skeins)
‥	light red 8196 (1 skein)
X	medium red 8198 (1 skein)
→	dark red 8202 (1 skein)
I	pink 8252 (1 skein)
□	light blue 8684 (9 skeins)
T	medium blue 8688 (1 skein)
/	pale apple green 9092 (1 skein)
\	medium apple green 9094 (1 skein)
Λ	light green 9100 (1 skein)
L	medium green 9102 (1 skein)
■	black 9800 (1 skein)

Napkin ring only

□	light blue 8684 (1 skein)
T	medium blue 8688 (1 skein)
→	dark red 8202 (1 skein)
I	pink 8252 (1 skein)
9	brown 8106 (1 skein)

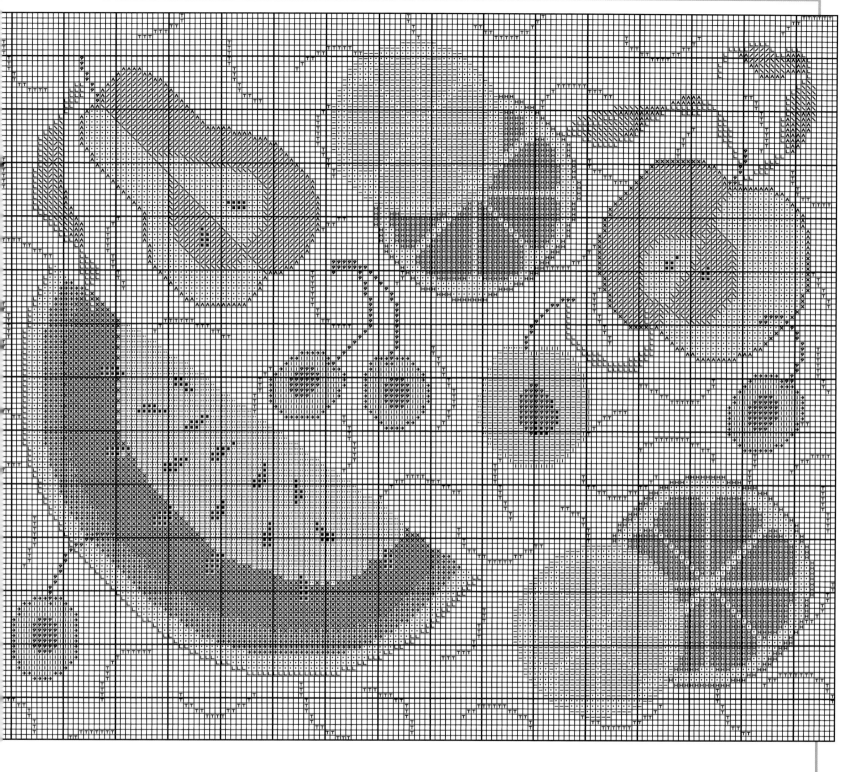
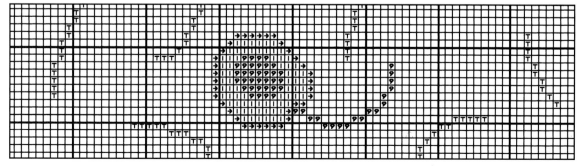

IRIS BOOK COVER

CHRISTINA MARSH

~

BEAUTIFUL MAJESTIC IRISES WERE A SOURCE OF GREAT INSPIRATION FOR THE ARTIST MONET, AND HE INCLUDED THEM IN MANY OF HIS PAINTINGS. MONET WAS A KEEN GARDENER AND GREW MANY DIFFERENT VARIETIES OF IRIS IN HIS WONDERFUL GARDEN AT GIVERNY. THE GARDEN STILL EXISTS AND THE RANGE NOW INCLUDES MANY IRIS HYBRIDS. THIS DESIGN WAS INSPIRED BY MODERN BI-COLOURED BEARDED IRISES, WHICH NOW GROW IN GREAT PROFUSION IN MONET'S GARDEN.

FINISHED SIZE

Front cover/picture 30.5 x 22.5 cm (12 x 9 in)

MATERIALS

Either 40.5 x 66 cm (16 x 26 in) of 12-guage mono
   interlock canvas for the book cover, *plus* the width
   of the spine (add this to the width, 66 cm/26 in)
or 40.5 x 32.5 cm (16 x 13 in), when stitched as a
   picture
No 20 tapestry needle
Tapestry wool in the colours given in the key
30.5 x 22.5 cm (12 x 9 in) book (you can add a
   border around the picture to alter the dimensions);
   the width of the spine does not matter, as long as
   you allow sufficient canvas and background wool

Opposite: stitch this attractive cover for a treasured book, or make a beautiful picture for your wall.

INSTRUCTIONS

1 For the picture, find the centre of the canvas by counting or by folding it in half, then half again, and making a single stitch where the folds cross. For the book cover, divide the canvas into five sections as shown in the diagram, and work the design in the second box from the right-hand side.

2 Mount the canvas in a tapestry frame, making sure it is evenly tensioned. Starting at the centre point, work the design in continental tent stitch, following the symbols on the chart and key.

3 When you have stitched the flowers and leaves, start the background, preferably working in diagonal rows (basketweave) as this will minimize distortion and make the stitching more even.

IRIS BOOK COVER KEY

Anchor Tapisserie wool

●	white 8000 (3 skeins)
T	light yellow 8038 (1 skein)
X	medium yellow 8040 (1 skein)
⌐	pink 8412 (1 skein)
I	cerise 8488 (1 skein)
V	light lilac 8584 (1 skein)
O	medium lilac 8590 (1 skein)
■	dark lilac 8592 (1 skein)
☐	medium blue green 8972 (21 skeins, this includes 18 skeins for the back cover and flaps)
/	dark blue green 8974 (3 skeins)
−	pale apple green 9094 (2 skeins)
K	light green 9098 (2 skeins)
Z	medium green 9102 (2 skeins)
◤	dark green 9120 (1 skein)

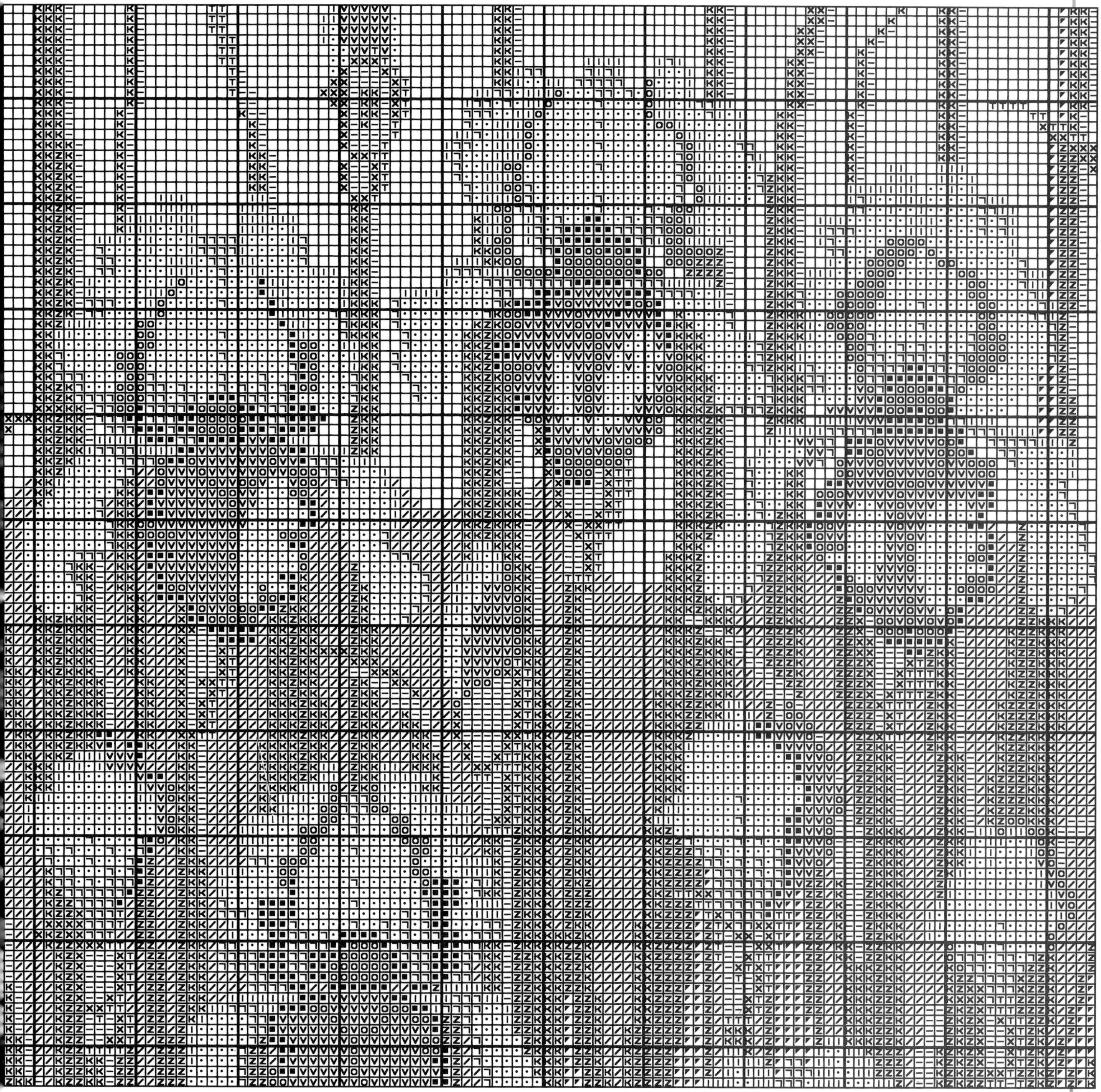

4 Stitch the back and the two flaps in diagonal tent stitch. You may prefer to use a different stitch, such as long and short stitch, which is quicker to embroider and requires less wool.

5 Remove work from the frame and stretch the canvas if necessary. Trim away surplus canvas, leaving a 12 mm (½ in) border of unworked canvas around the work. Fold over the unworked canvas allowances on each side and slipstitch (using sewing cotton) to the back of the embroidery.

6 Fold the 5 cm (2 in) flaps over and oversew the top and bottom edges securely. Finally, insert the book by placing the front and back covers into the flaps.

IRIS BOOK COVER KEY

•	white 8000
T	light yellow 8038
X	medium yellow 8040
⌐	pink 8412
I	cerise 8488
V	light lilac 8584
O	medium lilac 8590
■	dark lilac 8592
☐	medium blue green 8972
/	dark blue green 8974
−	pale apple green 9094
K	light green 9098
Z	medium green 9102
◤	dark green 9120

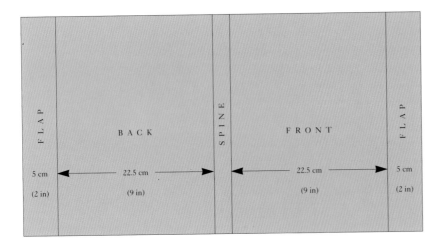

FLAP

BACK

SPINE

FRONT

FLAP

5 cm
(2 in)

22.5 cm
(9 in)

22.5 cm
(9 in)

5 cm
(2 in)

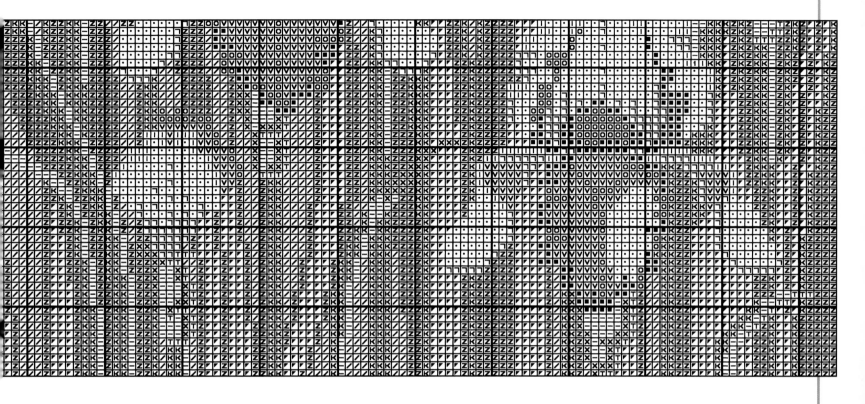

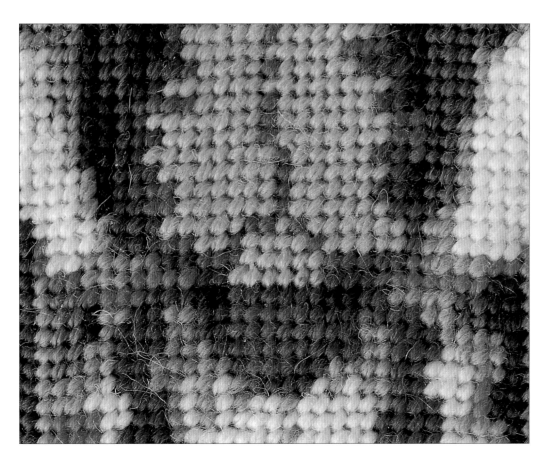

NEEDLEWORK TREASURY

*A few accessories that you have embroidered for yourself make
needlework all the more enjoyable as a pastime, so spoil yourself and
choose from this selection – a charming needlecase, a pincushion, a
spectacles case with a marine theme, and a pretty needlework box.*

ERSARI NEEDLECASE

MARCIA PARKINSON

T HE BASIC PATTERN FOR THIS NEEDLECASE WAS INSPIRED BY A FRAGMENT OF A TURKOMAN RUG, PROBABLY WOVEN IN THE LATE 18TH CENTURY BY TRIBAL ERSARI WEAVERS IN THE MOUNTAINS OF CENTRAL ASIA, WHILE THE COLOURS I HAVE USED IN THE NEEDLECASE REMIND ME OF THE VIVID BLUE AND SOFT GOLDS SEEN IN THE PAINTED WALLS OF THE JARDIN MAJORELLE IN MARRAKECH, MOROCCO.

FINISHED SIZE

21.5 x 16.5 cm (8½ in x 6½ in)

MATERIALS

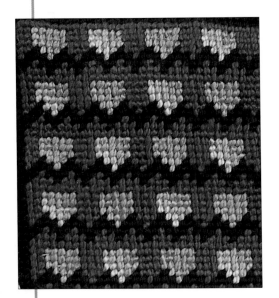

30 x 25 cm (12 x 10 in) of 13-gauge mono interlock canvas

No 22 tapestry needle

Embroidery threads in colours as given in the key

25 x 20 cm (10 x 8 in) of medium-weight cotton fabric, for lining the needlecase

2 pieces of navy felt, each 18.5 x 14 cm (7½ x 5½ in)

18.5 x 14 cm (7½ x 5½ in) of net (to hold tapestry needles)

Navy sewing thread

Large bead, for fastening

Opposite: this pretty needlecase will hold sufficient needles for all occasions and will last the stitcher's lifetime.

INSTRUCTIONS

1 Note that you have only 4 cm (1½ in) of canvas to spare around the finished work, so take some time to make sure your stitched area will sit in the centre of the canvas. You may find it easier to mark the centre line of the canvas and work the central row of the pattern first, then build up the pattern from this point.

2 Following the chart and key, embroider the design in half cross stitch. When you have completed the needlepoint, you may need to stretch the finished embroidery to make sure that it is a perfect rectangle.

3 Trim the finished embroidery to leave 12 mm (½ in) of unworked canvas on all sides, and trim the lining fabric to match.

4 Put the right side of the lining to the right side of the needlework. Machine stitch around three sides, stitching close to the embroidery. Trim surplus fabric from the corners

5 Turn the case right side out, then fold in the allowances along the open edge and slipstitch the opening.

6 Centre the two pieces of felt and the piece of net over the lining side of the needlecase. Baste and machine down the centre, attaching the pieces to the needlecase like book pages.

ERSARI NEEDLECASE KEY

DMC embroidery threads

No 3 perle cotton

- ⊡ bright blue 797 (2 skeins)
- ⊟ dark yellow 783 (1 skein)
- ◸ light gold 677 (1 skein)
- ⧄ medium gold 3046 (1 skein)
- ◼ dark gold 729 (1 skein)

Soft cotton embroidery thread

- ⊠ navy 2823 (2 skeins)

7 Using blue and gold threads, make the cord for the edge of the needlecase (see page 74). To attach the cord to the case, start stitching the cord in the middle of a short side, leaving a free end of around 10 cm (4 in). Continue attaching the cord around the outside of the needlecase until you reach the starting point again, then securely stitch through the two ends of the cord.

8 Tie a tidy knot in the two ends, leaving a loop big enough to pass over the bead. Unravel the cord below the loop and trim the ends to form a tassel.

9 Securely attach the bead to the other side of the needlecase, so that it will slip through the cord loop to make a fastening.

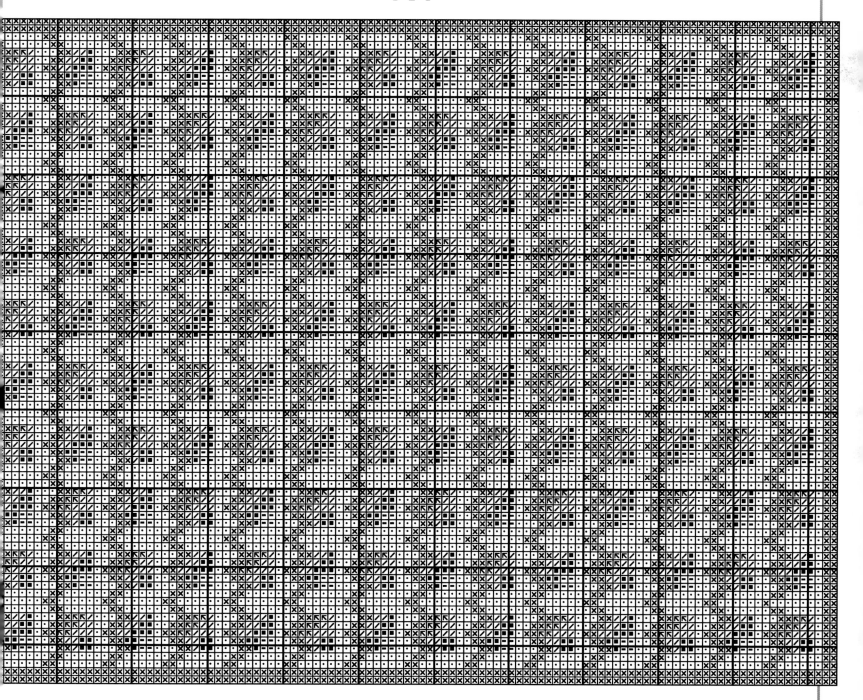

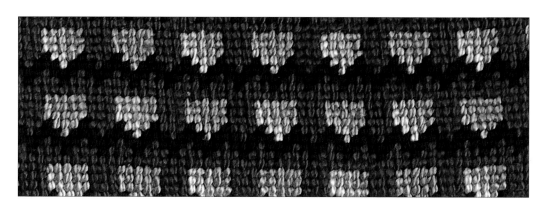

PINCUSHION & SPECTACLES CASE

KELLY FLETCHER

~

S MALL CREATURES OF ALL SHAPES, SIZES, COLOURS AND TYPES PROVIDE ENDLESS INSPIRATION FOR DESIGNS. THE LADYBIRD, WITH HER NATURALLY BRIGHT COLOURING GAVE ME THE OPPORTUNITY TO DESIGN A PINCUSHION USING SPOTS AND STRIPES TOGETHER. BRIGHTLY COLOURED TROPICAL FISH ARE ANOTHER FASCINATING, AND INDEED FANTASTIC, SIGHT — THE DESIGN OF THE CASE CAPTURES SOME OF THE COLOUR AND VARIETY OF SHAPES OF THESE FISH, AND THERE IS AN ELEGANT SEAHORSE ON THE OTHER SIDE.

FINISHED SIZE

Ladybird pincushion: 15 cm (6 in) square
  approximately
Sea creatures spectacles case: 9.5 x 18 cm (3¾ x
  7¼ in)

MATERIALS (PINCUSHION)

25 cm (10 in) square of 10-gauge double-thread
  canvas
No 18 tapestry needle
Tapestry wool in the colours as given in the key
18 cm (7¼ in) square of backing fabric, to
  complement the needlepoint
Suitable filling
70 cm (¾ yd) of upholstery cord

*Opposite: a cheerful
pincushion and brightly
coloured spectacles case make
a colourful and practical duo
to keep beside you as you
stitch.*

INSTRUCTIONS (PINCUSHION)

1 Decide where on the chart you would like to begin, and find the corresponding place on your canvas, remembering that the design should be centred on the canvas, leaving a 5 cm (2 in) border all round.

2 Thread your needle with wool no longer than 40 cm (16 in) – do not be tempted to cut the lengths longer than this or it will become very thin during stitching.

3 Following the symbols on the chart and key, complete the design in half cross stitch. Each square on the chart represents one stitch on your canvas.

4 When the design is completed, stretch the canvas if it has become distorted during stitching.

5 Elaborate finishing would destroy the charm of a small project like this one, so I suggest a very simple approach. First trim the edges of the unworked canvas to leave an allowance of 1.5 cm (⅝ in) all around.

6 With right sides facing, pin the backing fabric to the embroidered canvas around three sides of the pincushion, then baste and machine stitch these three sides, going as close as possible to the edge of the needlepoint.

7 Turn the canvas and fabric right sides out, and insert your chosen filling – really pack it in! – to create a very firm cushion. Hand stitch the final edge.

8 As an attractive and quick finishing touch, I added some gold braid – it looks very smart, especially with decorative corners.

9 On completion, stick the pins you used for step 6 into your pincushion and proceed to congratulate yourself for having made such a useful item!

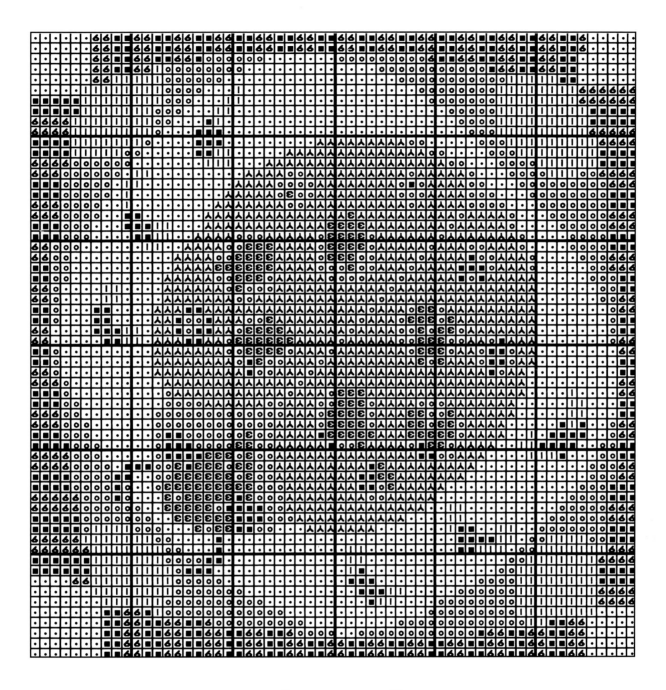

PINCUSHION KEY

Anchor Tapisserie wool

■	pale old gold 8006 (1 skein)	6	bright fuchsia 8526 (1 skein)
I	pale yellow orange 8114 (1 skein)	Ɛ	pale lilac 8586 (1 skein)
⅄	deep cyclamen 8440 (1 skein)	•	jade 8966 (1 skein)
		O	darkest chocolate 9666 (1 skein)

MATERIALS (SPECTACLES CASE)

30 cm (12 in) square (minimum) of 14-gauge mono canvas

No 20 tapestry needle

Tapestry wool in the colours as given in the key

22.5 cm (9 in) square of suitable lining fabric

Sewing thread to match lining fabric

INSTRUCTIONS (SPECTACLES CASE)

1 Find a suitable place to start on the chart and, following the symbols on the chart and key, thread your needle with wool of the appropriate shade (use lengths no longer than 40 cm/16 in throughout).

2 Stitch the design, using half cross stitch. Each square on the chart represents one stitch on your canvas.

3 When the design is completed, stretch the canvas if it has become distorted.

4 Once the canvas has dried out after stretching, trim the edges to leave 12 cm (½ in) of unworked canvas all around the needlepoint.

5 Fold the unworked canvas to the wrong side of the needlepoint and iron it down.

6 With wrong sides together, place the lining fabric over the wrong side of the work so that it exactly covers the needlepoint area, fold the edges under, and then pin and stitch it neatly in place. Aim to have only one unstitched row of canvas showing along the edge of the stitched canvas.

7 Oversew along the top edge of the specs case, using tapestry wool, then fold the canvas in half vertically.

8 Neatly oversew down the sides and along the bottom edge of the canvas, stitching into the empty squares and keeping the sides lined up with each other.

SPECTACLES CASE

Anchor Tapisserie wool

☒	off-white 8004 (1 skein)
☐ (I)	palest amber 8092 (2 skeins)
☐ (T)	yellow orange 8118 (2 skeins)
☐ (Y)	rust orange 8166 (1 skein)
☐ (V)	cyclamen 8436 (2 skeins)
+	magenta 8488 (1 skein)
•	cornflower blue 8690 (3 skeins)
☐ (Z)	peacock green 8920 (1 skein)
☐ (3)	pale jade 8964 (1 skein)
↓	dark priest grey 9768 (1 skein)

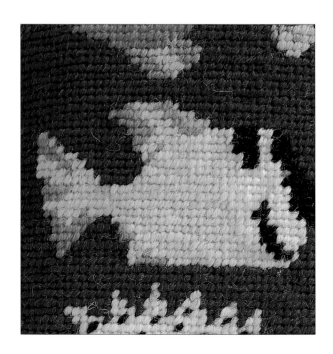

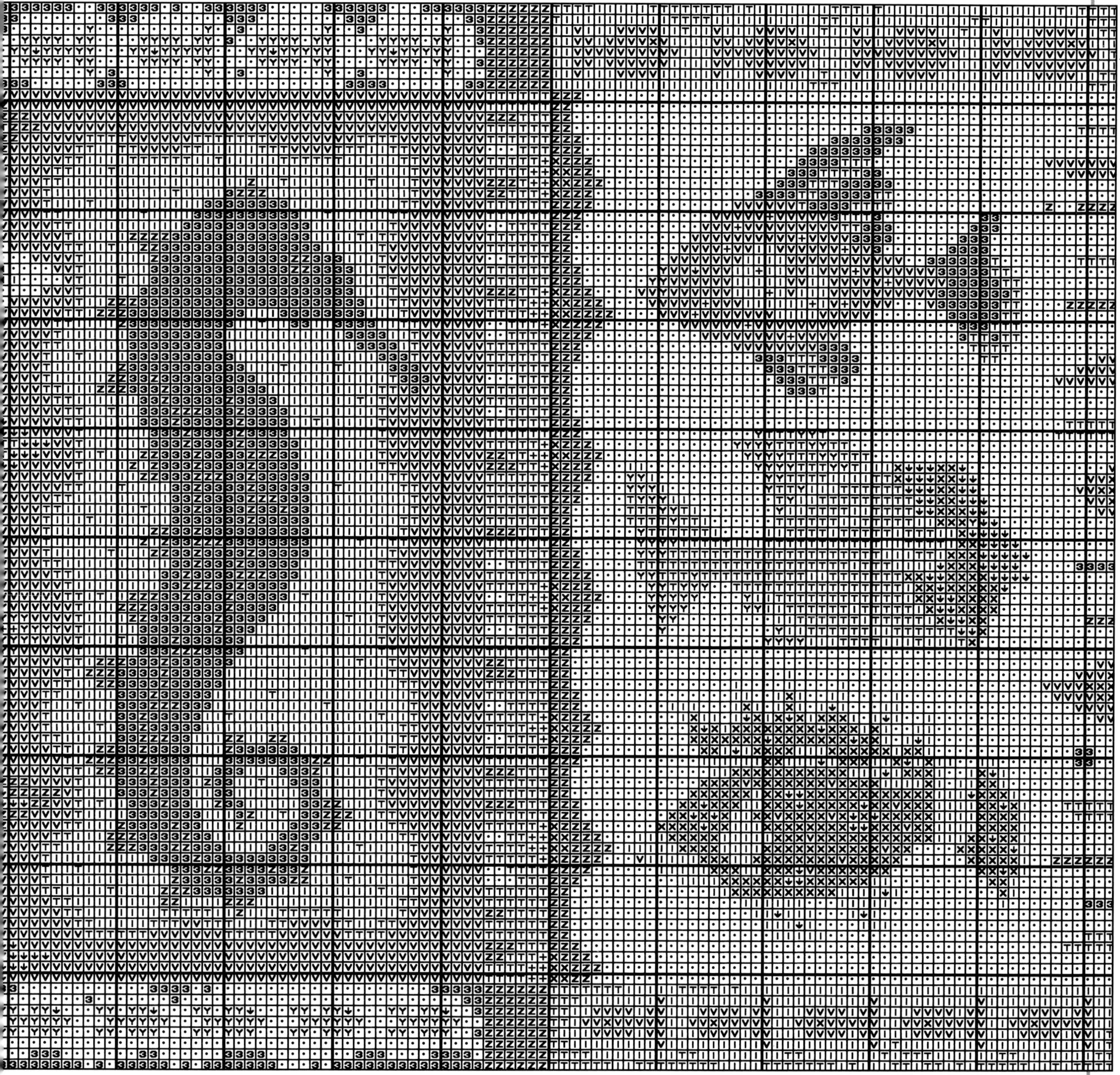

JACOBEAN-STYLE FOOTSTOOL

SANDRA HARDY

~

THIS DESIGN WAS INSPIRED BY WALL HANGINGS AND BED CURTAINS, DECORATED WITH CREWEL EMBROIDERY, TO BE FOUND IN THE VICTORIA AND ALBERT MUSEUM, LONDON. MANY OF THE RATHER FANCIFUL AND EXOTIC LEAVES AND FLOWERS SEEN IN JACOBEAN CREWEL WORK WERE TAKEN FROM THE PRINTED COTTONS BEING IMPORTED FROM INDIA. THIS DESIGN FEATURES A CENTRAL PANEL WITH A REPEAT BORDER; THERE IS NO DIRECTIONAL SLANT, AS IT IS VERY LIKELY TO BE VIEWED FROM ALL SIDES.

FINISHED SIZE

46 cm (18 in) square

MATERIALS

61 cm (24 in) of 14-gauge double-threaded canvas, in white

No 20 tapestry needle

Crewel wool in the colours given in the key

46 cm (18 in) square of lightweight polyester wadding

Staples and staple gun

40.5 cm (16 in) square of black calico

38 cm (15 in) square cushion pad for a wooden stool frame

Footstool (for suppliers, see page 141)

Opposite: the design, with its meandering flowers and stems and subtle colouring, is taken from crewel work embroidery, but needlepoint is more practical for a footstool.

INSTRUCTIONS

1 Mark the centre of the canvas; extend lines out to the edges, marking the centre of each side, and set the canvas in a frame.

2 Carefully counting out from the centre, start stitching the edges of the central panel, following the chart and the symbols in the key. Use half cross stitch and thread your needle with two strands of crewel wool (for two strands of Appletons, as used here, you will require only one strand of Paterna).

3 Complete all the motifs within the central square.

4 Next, stitch the border pattern, completing each quarter in turn and using the centre lines as a guide to correct positioning.

5 Finally, complete all the background, starting at the top and working downwards. This will help to keep the stitched areas as clean as possible.

6 Remove from the frame and continue as for the jewellery box lid (see page 32), pulling the needlepoint firmly for a good, smooth fit. When the cover is finally attached and the excess canvas cut away, staple a piece of black calico to cover the raw edges underneath the stool. Fix the seat pad back into the stool frame by means of the screws provided.

JACOBEAN-STYLE FOOTSTOOL KEY

Appletons crewel yarn

~	pale flame red 206 (2 skeins)
⧄	pale turquoise 524 (2 skeins)
⧓	medium turquoise 525 (2 skeins)
●	deep turquoise 527 (2 skeins)
⧅	pale sky blue 562 (2 skeins)
X	sky blue 564 (0.5 hank)
★	deep sky blue 567 (0.5 hank)
7	pale flesh tint 701 (0.5 hank)
◆	flesh tint 708 (0.5 hank)
■	dark china blue 748 (2 skeins)
Z	peacock blue 831 (2 skeins)
·	off-white 992 (2 hanks)

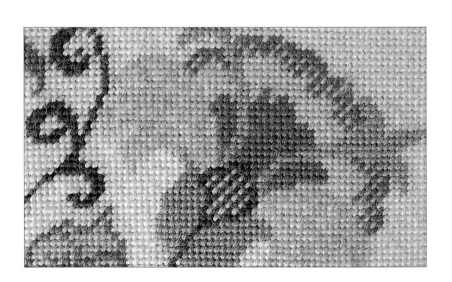

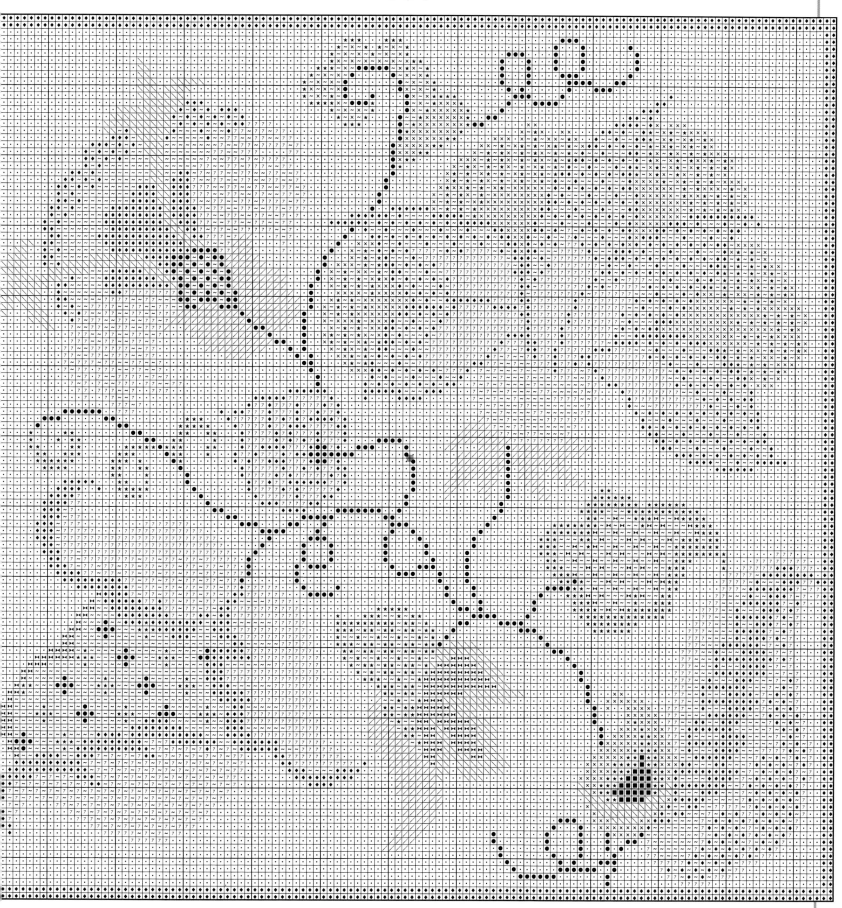

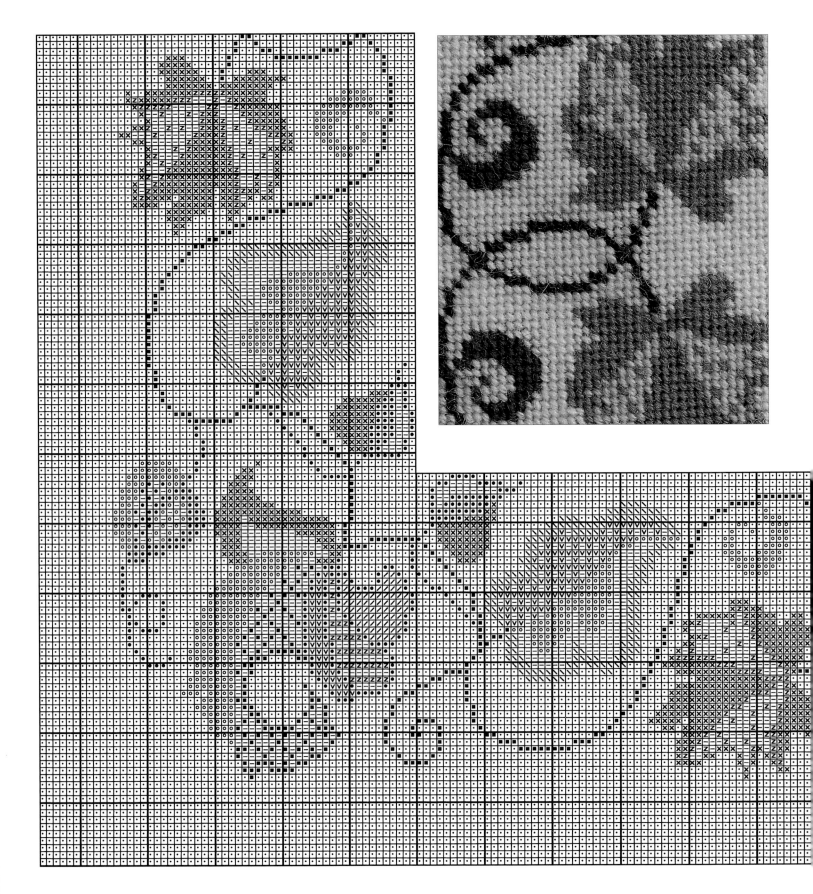

JACOBEAN-STYLE FOOTSTOOL KEY

Appletons crewel yarn

−	pale flame red 206
/	pale turquoise 524
V	medium turquoise 525
·	deep turquoise 527
\	pale sky blue 562
X	sky blue 564
O	deep sky blue 567
■	dark china blue 748
Z	peacock blue 831
•	off-white 992

GEOMETRIC NEEDLEWORK BOX

SANDRA HARDY

~

THIS LIVELY PATTERN WAS CREATED FROM A FADED SCRAP OF COTTON FABRIC FOUND ON A VICTORIAN BUTTON-BACK CHAIR. THE DESIGN PREDATES THE VICTORIANS, AS IT CAN BE SEEN ON SEVERAL 14TH-CENTURY DECORATED ISLAMIC MANUSCRIPTS. AN ATTRACTIVE LEAF MOTIF, TAKEN FROM ANOTHER FABRIC, HAS BEEN REVERSED AND ROTATED, THEN COLOURED WITH DIAGONAL LINES TO MAKE UP THE FINISHED PATTERN.

FINISHED SIZE

12.5 cm (5 in) square (needlepoint only)

MATERIALS

22 cm (9 in) square of 12-gauge interlock canvas, in white
No 18 tapestry needle
Tapestry wool in the colours given in the key
12.5 cm (5 in) square of lightweight polyester wadding
12.5 cm (5 in) square of cardboard
Crochet cotton
Large-eyed needle
Adhesive pads
Wooden box (for suppliers, see page 141), with a lid aperture of 12.5 cm (5 in) square

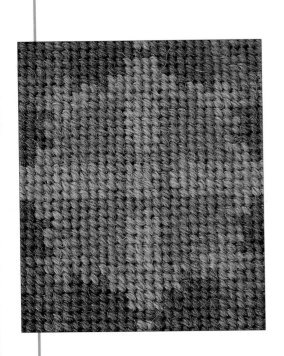

Opposite: colourful and pretty, this little box will hold embroidery scissors, tape and needles, but you could equally well use it as a trinket box for a dressing table.

INSTRUCTIONS

1 Mark the centre lines across the canvas in both directions with a permanent (waterproof) pen before setting it in a small frame.

2 Start stitching the design from the centre, following the symbols on the chart and key and using half cross stitch. Work outwards, completing both motifs and background areas together.

3 Remove from the frame and trim the unstitched canvas edges to 4 cm (1½ in) on all sides.

4 Place the canvas wrong side down on a flat surface. Centre the wadding over it, and then the card.

5 Using crochet cotton and the large-eyed needle, lace the canvas edges together over the back of the card.

6 When the lacing is completed, attach the needlepoint to the box lid, using adhesive pads.

GEOMETRIC NEEDLEWORK BOX
KEY

Anchor Tapisserie wool

⋈   purple 8528 (1 skein)

▪   pale lilac 8584 (1 skein)

Ƨ   palest periwinkle 8602 (1 skein)

▬   medium periwinkle 8606 (1 skein)

◆   deep periwinkle 8608 (1 skein)

◯   light peacock green 8916 (1 skein)

◉   peacock green 8918 (1 skein)

●   deep peacock green 8922 (1 skein)

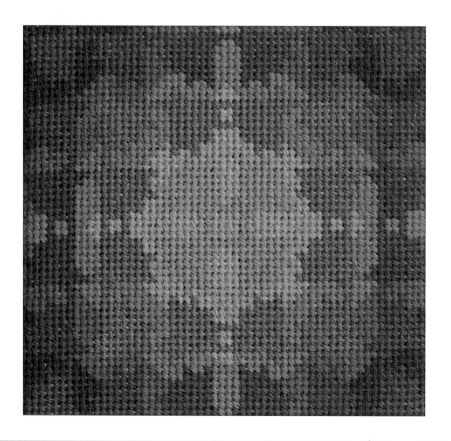

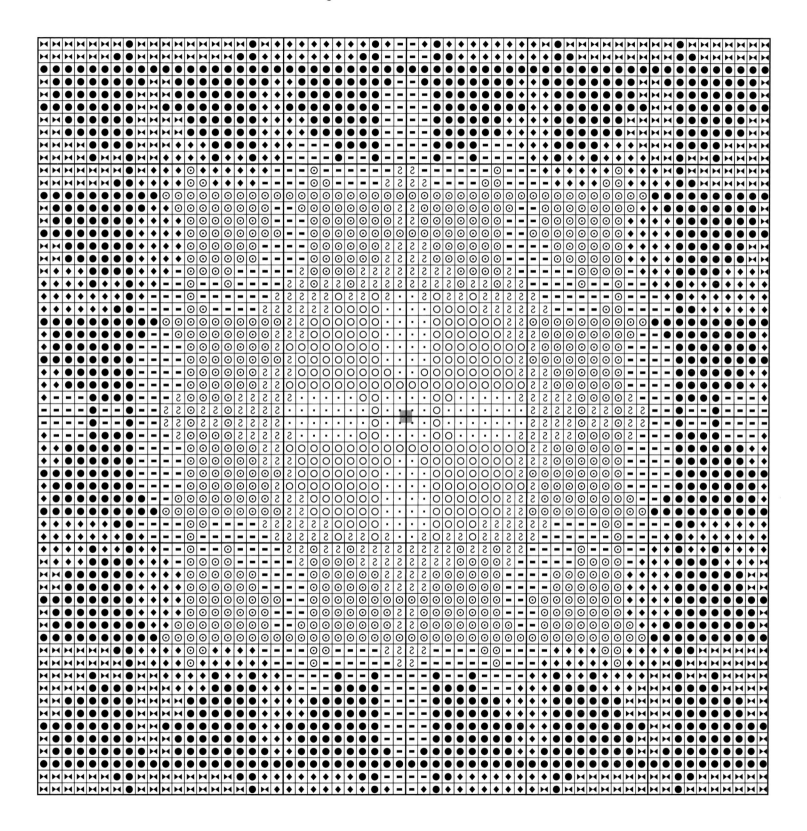

BASIC SKILLS

If you are new to needlepoint, you will be delighted to find that it is very easy to master the basic skills required. Along with each project in this book, you will find a detailed list of the materials required, including the type of canvas used and yarn quantities and colours. The only equipment you will need is a good pair of embroidery scissors and a frame (see below).

CANVAS

The fabric used for needlepoint embroidery is a fairly stiff evenweave canvas, with a specified number of threads or holes per 2.5 cm (1 in). Single or mono canvas has a weave of a certain number of threads per 2.5 cm (1 in). Interlocked canvas is similar, but here the threads are twisted so that they lock at intersections. Double (sometimes known as Penelope) canvas, is woven with pairs of threads running each way, and is graded according to the number of holes between pairs of threads.

The threads of a double canvas may be prised apart to make a fine single mesh for an area of extra fine stitching, as in the case of the bluebell picture, but for most designs it is possible to use either a single canvas or a double canvas, provided they have the same gauge (number of threads or holes per inch). It should be noted, however, that interlocked canvas tends not to be as hardwearing as the other types, and is therefore not so suitable for chair seats or footstools.

Other types of canvas used in this book include plastic canvas (Grape Vine Table Mat) and rug canvas (Camel Cushion).

YARNS

Fine embroidery yarns have been used for a few projects, but most of the items in this book were stitched with either tapestry yarn or crewel wools, the yarns traditionally used for needlepoint. Crewel wools have the advantage of being formed from strands that can be separated for finer work. The key given with each project specifies the particular brand of yarn used to stitch that project. The brands of tapestry and crewel wool used – Anchor, DMC and Paterna – come in very wide colour ranges, but the ranges are not identical and it is therefore best, if possible, to use the stated brand. If this is not readily available, however, or you have a particular preference for a specific brand, you will find conversion charts on page 142. These list alternative shades that might be suitable in the other brands, but it should be remembered that these are only suggestions. Ideally, it would be best to go to the shop and study the colours in the wool, bunching the skeins together as you go through the list to check that you are happy with the combination.

TAPESTRY NEEDLES

The size of needle required is specified with each project. A tapestry needle has a large eye that will carry the thread easily and a point that is blunted, so that it does not split the canvas or the threads of previous stitches. It is important to use a size of needle that will carry the yarn easily, but is not so thick that it will distort the canvas mesh during stitching.

FRAMES

The diagonal stitches used for most needlepoint, including the projects in this book, tend to pull the canvas gradually out of shape as you stitch. You can generally stretch it back into shape, as described below, but the majority of stitchers (though not all) prefer to use a frame to hold their work as they stitch. This minimizes the inevitable distortion and also makes it easier to form stitches correctly.

If you are stitching your first needlepoint, and do not wish to invest in a frame at this stage, it is possible simply to pin the work either to the back of a picture frame or to a pair of artists' stretchers, available from art supply shops.

The type of frame traditionally used for this work is a slate (roller) frame, which consists of two roller bars, which form the top and bottom of the frame and have webbing attached along their length, and two side pieces, which slot into the rollers at the top and bottom and are held with either split pins or wood screws. Some frames are attached to stands, for greater ease of stitching, while the simpler versions are propped against a table during stitching to leave both hands free.

The travel frame is a lightweight version of the slate or roller frame; it is easier to dismantle and carry around, but does not hold the canvas quite so firmly.

Any excess length of canvas can be rolled up on a slate or travel frame, but the webbing of the roller bars must be sufficiently wide to carry the entire width of the canvas.

Dressing a Roller Frame

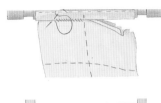

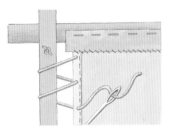

PREPARATION

Before you begin to stitch, you should prepare your canvas. The canvas sizes specified with projects in this book all include a margin around the finished work, to allow for attaching the canvas to a frame and for finishing. Canvas edges can be rough on hands and can fray wool, so if you are not using a frame you should either cover the edges before you begin with binding or with masking tape, or turn under and baste a narrow hem.

The needlepoint design must be centred on the canvas, to leave an even margin all around, and as a general rule designs are stitched from the centre outwards, so it is also helpful mark the centre of the canvas by basting central vertical and horizontal lines across it.

DRESSING A SLATE FRAME
You will require the
(unassembled) frame, your
canvas, with the centre lines
marked, webbing or strong tape
to go down each side of the
canvas, strong button thread and
needle, and either fine, strong
string or a heavy crochet cotton
and a large-eyed needle.
First stitch a strip of webbing or
strong binding tape down each
side edge, then turn under a
narrow hem along the top and
bottom edges, keeping the
centres marked. Matching the
centre point of the canvas edge
with the centre point of the
webbing on the roller, pin and
stitch the canvas to the webbing
along the top roller, working
from the centre outwards, and
using slanting oversewing
stitches, as shown. Repeat,
attaching the bottom edge of the
canvas to the bottom roller.

Fit the rollers into the side
pieces, rolling up any spare
canvas on the top and bottom
and leaving the centre exposed
for stitching. (The frame will
need to be dismantled and re-
assembled to expose unstitched
areas as work progresses.) Make
sure the frame is rigid and the
canvas is held taut.

Using string or strong thread,
lace the sides of the canvas over
the side edges of the frame,
stitching through the webbing at
intervals of about 2.5 cm (1 in)
and carrying the thread around
the sides. Knot the string
securely at the top of the frame.

STITCHING
Use a thread about 40 cm (16 in)
long when stitching. If you use a
longer thread you will find that
it may wear thin as you pull it
through the canvas holes.
Canvaswork stitches are made in
two separate movements,
inserting the needle down with
the top hand and pushing it up
with the lower hand; scooping
stitches, made with an all-in-one
movement, should be avoided as
they will tend to distort the
canvas.

To start stitching, make a knot
at the end of the thread and take
the needle down through the
work a short distance away from
your first (upward starting)
stitch. As you work towards the
knot, the thread will be secured
at the back of the work by the
stitches you are making. Trim off
the knot when you reach it with
your stitches. To finish, run your
thread through a line of stitches
at the back. Where areas of the
same colour are fairly close to
each other, you can carry the
thread through the back of other
stitches, but if they are some
distance away it is better to start
and finish separately.

Tent stitch

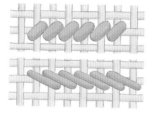

Also known as continental tent
stitch, this has been used for
several of the projects in this
book. It is sometimes used in
conjunction with basketweave,
or diagonal tent stitch, the
former being used for motifs,
and the latter for background
areas. Tent stitch produces a

very hard-wearing fabric as it
forms long slanting stitches at
the back of the work which
provide extra padding.

When you have finished one
row, working from right to left,
turn the frame upside down so
that you can also work the return
row from right to left. Continue
to stitch in this way. It is easy for
beginners to slip into half cross
stitch, so check the back of the
work from time to time, to make
sure that you are forming long
slanting stitches at the back, not
little verticals.

Diagonal tent stitch (basketweave)

This is a useful stitch for
background areas, as it causes
less distortion of the fabric than
tent stitch. Work the first row
from the top left down to the
bottom right, and then work the
next, interlocking row, back
upwards, forming a basketweave
effect at the back of the work.

Half cross stitch

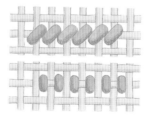

Worked from left to right with
small diagonal stitches, this
looks like tent stitch from the
front, but forms short vertical
stitches at the back and is
therefore not so hard-wearing as

tent stitch. If you wish to
substitute tent stitch for half
cross stitch, perhaps because you
are using a particular design for
an item such as a chair seat, you
will use almost twice as much
yarn.

Long and short stitch

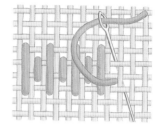

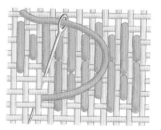

This consists of alternating long
and short stitches, arranged in
interlocking rows, and makes an
interesting variation to use as a
background stitch. Starting at
the top left, bring the needle up
and over four (or six) threads and
then down, then bring it out
next to the first stitch but one
thread up and take it over two
(or four) threads, continuing in
this way to the end of the row.
Work the subsequent row from
right to left, so that short stitches
are placed beneath the long
stitches of the previous row and
vice versa.

Oversewing
The edges of the Grape Vine
table mat, which is stitched on
plastic canvas, are oversewn,
stitches being taken through the
last row of holes at the edge of
the work and over the outer

covered. Canvas edges may be joined together in a similar way by folding back the spare canvas, leaving one unworked canvas thread at each edge; whipping the edges together with a neutral-coloured thread (matching up the edges carefully), and then working tent or half cross stitch along the join.

STRETCHING

Even if you use a frame, you may find that your finished needlepoint is not quite straight and needs to be stretched (blocked) into shape. This will generally succeed in pulling the work back into shape and will also improve its appearance. The dampness softens the stiffening in the canvas, making it malleable, and it can then dry and become stiff again in the correct shape.

You will need a board larger than the canvas (you will be putting pins or tacks into it, so don't use a good table); sheets of old newspaper or a cloth, a sheet of paper with the outline of your embroidery, either drawing pins (for small pieces) or brass or stainless steel pins or tacks and a hammer, and a laundry spray.

Using a waterproof pen or a pencil, start by drawing the outline of your finished piece (the desired shape, not the distorted one) on a piece of paper. Mark the centre lines across it both ways, to match the basted guidelines on your canvas. Use a set square (T-square) to check that corners have been drawn accurately (note that in a square or rectangle, the diagonals should be the same measurement). Lay sheets of newspaper or blotting paper or the cloth over your board and dampen them with the laundry spray.

Lay the outline drawing over the dampened surface, and then lay the embroidery, right side up, over the outline. You may also dampen the back of the needlepoint slightly. Matching the centre points of the embroidery to the outline drawing, pin both to the board. Place pins in the unworked canvas, just beyond the stitching, starting at the centre and working outwards to each corner and placing pins at intervals of approximately 2.5 cm (1 in) or less. When you have pinned the top edge, matching up the corners of the embroidery and outline, pin the bottom in the same manner.

Match up the sides and pin them in the same way, then leave the canvas to dry out naturally. If, after two or three days, it is still slightly distorted when unpinned, repeat the process.

MITRING CORNERS

You will often wish to mitre the corners of a finished needlepoint, either over a board (see below) or before adding a suitable backing fabric. To mitre a corner, first trim away spare canvas across the corner, leaving about 1 cm ($\frac{3}{8}$ in) of canvas extending beyond the corner of the stitchery (or the mounting board).

Next, fold the cut edge over to the back of the work. Bring the sides together at the back to make a diagonal join at the corner, which can then be stitched to hold it in place.

LACING AND MOUNTING

If an embroidery is to be set in a

frame, it will need to be mounted over hardboard or a heavy cardboard. You will require a piece of board cut to the size of the finished embroidery, drawing pins (thumb tacks), strong thread or crochet cotton, and a large-eyed needle. When choosing the frame and board, bear in mind that the board should fit loosely in the frame, to allow for the extra bulk of the canvas edges. Some people like to place a layer of lightweight polyester wadding over the upper surface of the board, to back the embroidery.

Lay the embroidery over the board, matching centre points, and pin it to the top edge of the board, working from the top centre outwards. When you have pinned the top edge in place, pin the bottom edge and then the sides. Take the unworked canvas to the back of the board. You can either fold over the top and bottom edges and then the

Mitring corners

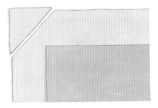

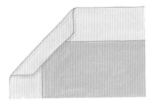

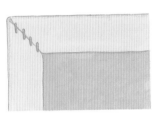

Lacing and mounting

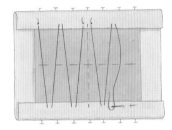

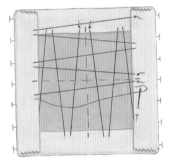

sides or, for a neater finish at the back, you can mitre the corners, as shown above.

Take a long length of thread and secure it at the centre top allowance of the work. Lace from top to bottom and back up again, out to one side, taking up several canvas threads at each stitch, to avoid pulling threads out. Fasten the thread off temporarily and, taking a new length of thread and starting at the centre top again, work out to the other side.

Remove the pins from the top and bottom edges of the board, then go to the lacing and work out to each side again, pulling each stitch tighter to take up any slack. Fasten the threads securely at the ends.

Repeat the process with the side edges.

Yarns and fabrics

UK

Appleton Bros Ltd, Thames Works, Church Street, Chiswick,
London W4 2PE
Telephone: 0181 994 0711

Coats Paton Crafts (for Anchor yarns), McMullen Road,
Darlington, Co Durham DL1 1YQ
Telephone: 01325 381010

DMC Creative World Ltd, Pullman Road, Wigston, Leics
LE18 2DY
Telephone: 0116 2811040

The Craft Collection Ltd, Paterna Persian tapestry yarn and
Readicut Wools, Terry Mills, Westfield Road, Horbury WF5 9SA
Telephone (24-hour orders): 01924 811800

USA

Access Commodities (for Appleton yarns), PO Box 1355, Terrell,
TX 75160
Telephone: 972 563 3313

Potpourri etc (for Appleton yarns), 209 Richmond Street, El
Segundo, CA 90245; Telephone: 310 322 8512

Coats & Clark (for Anchor yarns), PO Box 24998, Greenville SC
29616
Telephone: 800 243 0810

The DMC Corporation, Port Kearney Bld, #10 South Kerney, NJ
07032-0650
Telephone: 201 589 0606

Paternayan JCA Inc, 35 Scales Lane, Townsend, MA 01469

AUSTRALIA

Penguin Threads Pty Ltd (for Appleton yarns), 25/27 Izett Street,
Prahran, Victoria 3181
Telephone: 03 9529 4400

Coats Spencer Crafts (Anchor yarns), Level 1, 382 Wellington
Road, Mulgrave, Victoria 3170
Telephone: 03 9561 2288

DMC (Australia) Pty Ltd, PO Box 317, Earlwood,
NSW 2206
Telephone: 02 9559 3088

Stadia Handcrafts (for Appleton and Paterna yarns),
PO Box 357, Beaconsfield, NSW 2014; Telephone: 02 9565 4666

Kits

Jolly Red, Lynwood, The Green, Hambridge TA10 0AT
Telephone: 01460 281809

Russell House Tapestries, PO Box 12, Wiveliscombe,
Taunton, TA4 2YZ; Telephone: 01984 624135

Acknowledgements

The authors would like to thank the following people and companies: for supplying yarns and canvases, as
specified in the keys accompanying charted designs – Coats (Anchor yarns and canvases), DMC (DMC yarns
and Zweigart canvases), The Craft Collection (Paterna and Readicut yarns), and Appletons (sample skeins);
Maple Textiles, London (0181 778 8049) for seed beads; Luxury Needlepoint, Rye (01797 225145) for the
jewellery box (page 30); Eastfield Woodworks, Brough (01430 441231) for the key cupboard (page 92); Martin
Laudon, Northampton (01604 586144) for the Marrakech box (page 50) and needlework box (page 134);
(finished needlepoints can be fitted into the boxes if required); Russell House Tapestries, for the Kurd cushion
finishing kit (page 54); Cheshire Distribution (9 Springmount Hill, Northgate Road, Stockport, Cheshire SK3
0LX) and Poole Pottery Ltd (Poole, Dorset BH15 1RF), for giving permission to base a project on their designs
(page 92), and Remember When, Norwich (01508 489694) for the footstool (page 128).

Thread Conversions

The length of a skein varies between brands. The numbers in brackets beside certain shade numbers indicate the number of skeins required where this differs from the number given in the key.

Tapestry Wools

Herb Pillow

Anchor	DMC	Paterna
8006	ecru	764 (11)
8016	7727	773
8392	7200	964
8396	7133	915
8404	7139	900
8452	7804	913
8524	7253	322
8526	7255	321
8488	7153	322
8992	7909	620
9004	7542	D522
9006	7320	612
9094	7772	614
9180	7427	600

Lily of the Valley Frame

Anchor	DMC	Paterna
8000	blanc (2)	260 (2)
8012	7905 (4)	715 (4)
8394	7132	946
8434	7605	905
8588	7709	333
8644	7798	543
8686	7799	545
9018	7384	613 (3)

Victorian Jewellery Box

Anchor	DMC	Paterna
8002	white	263
8012	7905	715
8032	ecru	716
8054	7739	754
8734	7292	513
8736	7293	511
9004	7542	663
9112	7382	614
9114	7769	612
9534	7918	854

Birds in a Tree combined list

Anchor	DMC	Paterna
8038	7078	735 (2)
8092	7431 (5)	762 (6)
8094	7433	760 (2)
8152	7742	815 (2)
8252	7121 (10)	491 (11)
8292	ecru (2)	262 (2)
8326	7123	873 (2)
8418	7205	912 (2)
8602	7244 (6)	344 (7)
8786	7302 (10)	504 (11)
8966	7912	D502
9064	7870	534
9092	7549	624 (3)
9304	7361	653
9772	7300 (4)	256 (4)

Birds in a Tree Cushion

Anchor	DMC	Paterna
8038	7078	735 (2)
8092	7431 (5)	762 (6)
8094	7433	760 (2)
8152	7742	815 (2)
8252	7121 (10)	491 (11)
8292	ecru (2)	262 (2)
8326	7123	873 (2)
8418	7205	912 (2)
8602	7244	344 (5)
8786	7302 (10)	504 (11)
8966	7912	D502
9064	7870	534
9092	7549	624 (3)
9304	7361	653
9772	7300 (4)	256 (4)

Birds in a Tree Tieback

Anchor	DMC	Paterna
8038	7078	735
8092	7431	762
8094	7433	760
8152	7742	815
8252	7121	491
8292	ecru	262
8418	7205	912
8602	7244	344 (3)
8786	7302	504
9092	7549	624
9304	7361	653
9772	7300	256

Morning Glory Bell Pull

Anchor	DMC	Paterna
8114	7431 (3)	772 (3)
8486	7255	323 (4)
8490	7153	351
8644	7798 (5)	543 (5)
8690	7317 (2)	542 (2)
8990	7911	681 (3)
9006	7320	612 (3)
9018	7384 (3)	613 (3)
9218	7354	651
9800	noir	220 (12)

Marrakech Box

Anchor	DMC	Paterna
8058	7504	734
8104 (1)	7781 (1)	730
8424	7208 (1)	910
8426	7218	900
8530	7259	320
8792 (2)	7306 (2)	501
8822	7650	580
8990	7387	661
9002	7542	663
9028	7408	660
9800 (4)	Noir	220

Kurd Cushion

Anchor	DMC	Paterna
8058	7504	734
8062	7508	731
8204 (4)	7107 (4)	840
8402	7139	901
8424 (2)	7208	910
8736	7593	513
8740 (5)	7297	511
8742 (6)	7590 (7)	510
9216	7363	642
9798 (3)	7309	221

Crazy Cats Footstool

Anchor	DMC	Paterna
8032	blanc	260 (2)
8054	7503	735 (2)
8114	7431 (2)	773 (2)
8416	7204 (8)	932 (9)
8418	7205	912 (2)
8712	7715 (2)	D392 (2)
9162	7772	694 (4)
8510	7174	413
9636	7262	473
9774	7558	D391 (2)
9794	7705 (3)	D346 ((3)

Animal Numbers Picture

Anchor	DMC	Paterna
8000	blanc	260 (4)
8114	7431	773 (4)
8152	7742	815 (3)
8392	7132	964 (3)
8438	7136 (3)	943 (3)
8452	7151	963 (4)
8586	7241 (3)	333 (3)
8612	7247	571
8684	7800 (3)	505 (3)
8690	7797 (2)	541 (2)
8704	7715	213
8716	7292	211 (4)
8938	7861 (2)	D502 (2)
9092	7549	624
9192	7351	673

Tiger Pencil Case

Anchor	DMC	Paterna
8034	ecru	261
8114	7431	762
8202	7666	970
8212	7253	843
8392	7132	964
8524	7211 (2)	303 (2)
8688	7314	544
8918	7598	D502
9162	7772	694
9680	7236	D123

Primroses Chair Seat

Anchor	DMC	Paterna
8264	7447 (3)	860 (3)
8734	7605 (2)	905 (2)
9022	7387	610
9076	7370 (3)	604 (3)
9172	7422 (3)	695 (3)
9442	7452 (11)	445 (12)
9524	7455 (8)	803 (9)
9556	7175 (11)	883 (12)
9800	noir (21)	220 (23)

Teacup Cupboard

Anchor	DMC	Paterna
8012	7905	704
8016	7727	703
8018	7725	726
8032	ecru	263
8062	7474	732
8304	7762	845
8308	7851	844
8342	7179	492
8684	7799	545
8686	7798	544
8966	7542	D522
8984	7954	621
9634	7520	463
9678	7275	202
9772	7510	204

Irises and Poppies Cosy

Anchor	DMC	Paterna
8006	ecru	764
8012	7905	715
8036	7746 (5)	756 (5)
8114	7431	772
8202	7666 (3)	970 (3)
8590	7711	332
8592	7895	312
8602	7244	344
9006	7320 (2)	612 (2)
9100	7768	698 (3)
9120	7346	696
9152	7340	693
9800	noir	220

Foxglove Cushion

Anchor	DMC	Paterna
8114	7431	772
8434	7605	905 (3)
8488	7255	322
8490	7153 (3)	351 (3)
8526	7255 (3)	321 (3)
8528	7257	320 (2)
8786	7302	504 (3)
8790	7304	502
9022	7387 (5)	610 (5)
9094	7772 (3)	614 (3)
9096	7382	634 (3)
9100	7768	698
9786	7715	213
9800	noir	220

Summer Fruits Setting

Anchor	DMC	Paterna
8002	blanc	263
8106	7497	431
8116	7786 (2)	772 (2)
8168	7947 (2)	810 (2)
8196	7946 (2)	842 (2)
8198	7606 (2)	841 (2)
8202	7666 (2)	970 (2)
8252	7122	491
8684	7799 (12)	545 (13)
8688	7316	544
9092	7772 (2)	624 (2)
9094	7771	694
9100	7344 (2)	612 (2)
9102	7345	631
9800	noir	220

Iris Book Cover

Anchor	DMC	Paterna
8000	blanc (4)	260 (4)
8038	7453	735
8040	7724	942
8412	7202 (2)	913 (2)
8488	7153	353 (2)
8584	7896 (2)	314 (2)
8590	7895 (2)	332 (2)
8592	7708 (2)	331 (2)
8972	7943 (27)	681 (30)
8974	7906 (4)	D500 (4)
9094	7771 (2)	694 (2)
9098	7770 (3)	621 (3)
9102	7769 (3)	631 (3)
9120	7345 (2)	611 (2)

Pincushion

Anchor	DMC	Paterna
8006	ecru	263 (2)
8114	7431	773 (2)
8440	7136	942 (2)
8526	7255	301 (2)
8586	7241	333
8966	7912 (2)	D502 (2)
9666	7353 (2)	420 (2)

Spectacles Case

Anchor	DMC	Paterna
8004	blanc	260 (2)
8092	7431	762 (3)
8118	7435	772 (3)
8166	7740	812
8436	7104 (3)	944 (3)
8488	7153	353
8690	7797	541 (4)
8920	7861	D502 (2)
8964	7952 (2)	D503 (2)
9768	7624	221

Geometric Needlework Box

Anchor	DMC	Paterna
8528	7257	311
8584	7251	314
8602	7241	344
8606	7709	333
8608	7243	332
8916	7598	523
8918	7861	522
8922	7596	521

Trinket Box
No 5 perle cotton

Anchor	DMC
302	743
1212	782
45	814

Stranded cotton

681	3051
895	223

Soft cotton embroidery thread

0279	3819
0308	782
072	3685
0896	3803

Metallic gold thread

Bluebell Wood Picture
This was stitched in Paterna yarn which can either be used double-stranded, or separated into single strands, for the petit point. Alternatively, use either Appletons crewel wool (one strand for petit point and two strands for all other areas) or DMC stranded cotton (three strands for petit point and six strands for all other areas).

Anchor	DMC	Paterna
102	553	312
141	778	326
184	3772	472
202	951	405
202	950	474
203	3064	404
241	733	643
243	732	642
244	830	641
251	3012	653
251A	369	694
253	704	693
302	3773	473
403	987	611
421	989	613
452	554	304
472	745	704
547	904	690
551	445	673
604	3609	323
606	550	311
692	3047	755
822	792	341
841	472	644
872	3013	645
877	819	327
882	746	695
893	3747	334
894	340	333
895	333	332
987	762	256

Grape Vine Table Mat
Stranded cottons

Anchor	DMC
149	336
157	3807
175	794
176	793
210	376
214	368
216	320
240	966
386	746
1043	369

Ersari needlecase
No 3 perle cotton

Anchor	DMC
132	797
307	783
886	677
887	3046
890	729

Soft cotton embroidery thread

0152	2823

Jacobean-style footstool
Crewel embroidery yarn

Appletons	Paterna
206	491
524	523
525	522
527	521
562	585
564	503
567	501
701	494
708	874
748	571
831	D522
992	262

Index